365 REVOLUTIONS

CONTENTS

LEADERSHIP EMBODIED
—UCHENNA BAKER, PHD

To embody means to be an expression of or give a tangible or visible form to. Leadership embodied is ontological. Ontology is the philosophical study of being, becoming, and existing. What ontological inquiry calls for is the ongoing commitment to the discovery of who we are being. It calls for us to consider a paradigm where we do not have all the answers but rather, we are constantly engaging with the questions. The engaging invites us to remain present with how we are showing up in the world, how the world occurs for us, and ultimately discovering what our contribution to the world will be.

When one embodies leadership, they have access to every aspect of their being. This access is an invitation to interrogate one's assumptions and one's way of being in the world. Fear, doubt, and pain are often unearthed, and possibilities become available for the creation of something new. One then comes to discover that when they fearlessly invite possibilities for themselves, they open a world of possibilities for others.

This type of leadership is risky. It is vulnerable. To be human is to be afraid, to be angry, to hurt. But true leadership is about creating a new future. It is about creating and inviting new possibilities despite those human feelings of fear, anger and pain. Leadership that creates new possibilities cannot be created from a past-driven trajectory, lest it simply becomes an extension of the past. While we must honor the past, leaders are not called to recreate it. Leadership that creates new futures requires that we challenge our taken-for-granted assumptions about ourselves, others, and the world. It requires that we reconsider the limits and barriers we place on ourselves; and calls us to disrupt the social paradigms that assume racial, gender, and economic hierarchies.

This type of leadership requires a commitment to something bigger than oneself. It is risky and it is vulnerable. However, when individuals continuously make themselves available to the possibilities of creating futures that require their leadership, they become keenly aware of the world around them and can choose a life of freedom without limits. Individuals might then see themselves as part of the world around them rather than one who happens to simply exist within in it.

One might call my chance encounter with Lucas a divine intervention. Although we just met, we already knew each other. We understood what was at stake for the world. We knew that despite our flawed humanness we had something to offer. What Lucas offers in this book is revolutionary. He is creating new futures through poetry and yoga. In reading his work, one comes to understand the body as a vessel that carries years of historical trauma but also personifies resistance and resilience. We cannot separate the body from its past, but we have the power to create something new.

What flows through our bodies; what enters in and what has the capacity to flow out is an expression of power. Yoga invites us to lead our bodies. It is an exercise in testing our capacity to bend, twist, and fold the past within and expunge it out in each breath. Each breath offering a chance to be free. To be seen. To be heard. To regain power. Each breath is a voice, a battle cry for history and a call for the future. Our bodies, our voices, and our very existence is a form of resistance. We show up despite, we love, in spite of, and we generate in the face of opposition.

We embody the future.
We are the revolution.

FORWARD —MICHELLE CASSANDRA JOHNSON

Author of Skill in Action and
Finding Refuge: Heart Work for
Healing Collective Grief

We have endured a time when a virus emerged and called us to task. It has asked us if we value collective care, humanity and if we want to sustain the planet. The virus is quite clear in what it is uncovering. Coronavirus has forced us to reckon with all that is broken, all that is working as intended that must be dismantled, all of those who are unwell, and how our culture breeds a system of superiority deeming others inferior, and therefore unworthy of wellness. The reckoning upon us has dug up what many of us have known for quite some time-if we want to survive, we have to change our way of being. Our hearts, bodies, ecosystem, and planet have been stripped of humanity in the most gruesome ways. It is time for us to come back to the heart, body, and wholeness of who we are through our awareness of the reality that we are one collective body while we are in individual bodies. We are interconnected.

Amid Covid-19, a resurgence of the Black Lives Matter movement arose, although people had been calling for Black lives to matter well before the murders of Black and Brown people took place during the spring and summer of 2020. Some have been working to break down capitalism for centuries, and Covid-19 revealed how vulnerable many of us are, given capitalism has been designed to support only a few materially. Covid-19 attacked us all but disparately, affecting Black, Brown and poor people as well as our elders, the historical record keepers of our communities. These people contracted Covid-19 at a much higher rate due to the stress systemic racism, classism, ageism, and other forms of oppression placed on the body and nervous system. These systems of superiority made clear who is disposable and who is not. All of this happened in the context of ill-equipped hospitals and clinics while healthcare workers saw more death than they have ever encountered before.

This suffering occurred while wildfires blazed across large swaths of California, Colorado, Washington, and Oregon. It was as if the planet was saying the world has been on fire but let me show you how much. Let me show you how dire our situation is. The only thing that I am aware of that can meet this kind of suffering, planetary devastation, and loss is a spiritual practice. A practice that calls us back into our interconnectedness through self-study, reflection, connection, and action so we can recognize how to work to bring the planet back into balance. 365 Revolutions is a guide to supporting us in doing just that.

Lucas has written a book that calls us into deep embodiment, not for the purpose of transforming our physical shape or physical exercise. But instead to deepen our understanding of how we have been conditioned by dominant culture. To heighten our awareness of how we and others are suffering in our bones, tissues, muscles, and hearts. To unearth the things we would rather not reckon with. To become aware of the reality that we must change. Lucas calls us into action through the alchemy of prose, poetry, art, self-study, and movement. 365 Revolutions asks us to evolve by becoming part of the revolution taking place in our homes, spiritual spaces, yoga studios, workplaces, and streets as communities. The revolution is calling for us to acknowledge our history and the harm it has caused, to create systems of accountability and repair, so we can be better to one another.

This book is beautifully written and will cause the reader to pause and contemplate what toxicity they might be holding in their body while asking them to consider how they want to embody the values of justice and liberation for all. 365 Revolutions is an offering that will meet this moment-the reckoning we find ourselves in now and the aftermath before the healing. It is not a yoga book about posturing; it is a book about taking a stand against the forces intended to annihilate us and the planet. As Lucas describes in his introduction, this book is about warriorship. We do not need warriors who are impulsive or who carelessly use their power. Warriorship is about grace, strength, and wielding our power for a just cause. Allow the discomfort, pain, joy, resilience, curiosity, and discovery derived from your experience reading 365 Revolutions to steward you into warriorship so we can truly create a world where we are not bound by our suffering but instead by our freedom.

INTRODUCTION
—LUCAS SMIRALDO

There is a revolution waiting in the very bones of us, in our tissues, in our muscle memories and the daily pulse of us. That revolution extends centuries, back to 1619 and before, ahead toward a just world of belonging, one for which we catch glimpses. That world relentlessly cries for our full attention. These poems are revolutions to put into your body and they are cast in a full multiplicity of personas. I am a playwright, I am a poet, I am a yoga student, and my intent was to invite a daily practice that might confirm the difficult truths of our collective history, embody these understandings, and provoke the need for conscience, justice, and action.

This book is an act of imagination, constructed over four years, grounded in stories that rose as I placed my body and my mind's eye into each pose and waited and listened. Eventually the body took me into words and those words gathered into an intent, a song of sorts. I did my best to give each piece a full life, its full song, before moving to the next.

I own my positionality within that framework. I am a cisgender, straight white Jewish male who lives in a world that centers my identity every day, and advantages me in ways that are almost always to the detriment of everyone else. That is not an expression of guilt or shame. It is a reality that has defined this nation and the world for a very long time.

The yoga industry is an extension and a reflection of these realities and racism, sexism, and ableism need to be confronted and people who have been conspicuously missing from yoga culture and practices, explicitly affirmed, if we are to create the comprehensive healing spaces and sanctuaries that are desperately needed across this country and throughout the world. We can't get there with universal platitudes and evoking universal sisterhood and brotherhood while the suffering continues skirted and unnamed.

Let me animate the purpose behind these poems with a few examples.

Recently I saw a movie, "The Last Black Man in San Francisco" written by Joe Talbot, Robert Richert, and Jimmie Falls and directed by Mr. Talbot. In part, the movie interrogates the gentrification or "mass recolonization" of the previously black communities of San Francisco. Near the end of the film, Danny Glover, who plays a father to one of the two main lead characters, speaks about the shipyards and how black people were the ship builders (as was Toni Morrison's father) and had every right to claim San Francisco as their home and be recognized within its legacy. While writing poems for Sphinx Pose or Sālamba Bhujangāsana, I imagined the pose as a view over the bow of a ship, a view of the "Maafa" or great calamity of the middle passage and onto the ship builders as they construct vessels of resistance and of liberation.

My bones know
the deck
whether wood
or iron.

I am prone
to no soft landing,
and to coastal crests,
and restive winds
and harbors

that were anything
but safe to me.

Once forced below
I took my hour of light
and made it
into
centuries.

I stared down
the leaping waters
and did not
leave my
breath
I won this lift
and vision

from the tower
of my ribs
and whispered
to my children
to weld another/deck

to seek
a different bay
to fire up the
steel
to liberate this vessel.

Other buried narratives found their way into the body of the work. I believe I was holding the residue of a searing presentation offered by Amber Sterud Hayward, Language Director for the Puyallup Tribe of Indians, hosted in Tacoma's City Council Chambers for city employees.

Ms. Hayward's presentation, grounded in over seventy interviews of victims and descendants, laid out the horrendous legacy of the Cushman Indian Boarding School, which like many of its kind across the United States, was designed for the purpose of extinguishing the identities of Puyallup and other Salish children and forcefully separating them from their families.

The legacies of those schools, history of genocide, survivance and resilience of Native American people is expressed in this poem inspired by *Sūcirandhrāsana* or *Eye of the Needle* pose near the end of the book:

We are the people
who reach for
the eye of the dawn
though you forced
our welted backs onto boarding school
beds.

We kept our tongues
deep in our throats
where you could not

hear the language
swimming there.

We made our thighs
strong
by pulling the
morning toward them.

We tucked our bodies
into a survival
knot
that you could not
untwist.

We stretched our fingers
toward the fire
and this light
threads now

the narrow open spaces
like summer
on dead winter ground.

The occupation stories
are coming to their feet,
we have stretched them
ready

until we strike
the earth
like hided sticks
and bring
a rising.

I also invite a new consideration of
whiteness, of what race has meant for
us, of what we gain, and of the humanity
we lose, if we ignore the structural racism
that bolsters our position at the expense
of just about everyone else. These poems
are not a call to the deep indulgences
of guilt, but toward the greater call for
awareness and responsibility. What better
way to start than to infuse that call into
our daily physical practices? This is what
I had in mind when I wrote this piece
inspired by *Utthita Hastāsana in Tāḍāsana*
or *Mountain with Extended Arms.*

I stand
among those
of us
who have always
done
but never been,
the named,
the titled

the rush the din

the unlistening
steep of my back,
the towers I gaze from
the fore of my head,

the air between us,
the snows without a listener,
this life of blind and bound ascendance

and all I yet
would gain
without
my saying.

I recently attended a "remote" retreat with Michelle Johnson, a yoga teacher, activist, consultant who is living as both a healer and freedom fighter, and it became clear to me during that workshop, that Michelle is deeply driven by love as an active verb and by the call to accountability. In this spirit, Michelle has written the book, "Skill in Action", which evokes the call to warriorship as embodied by Arjuna who was called to this very engagement by Krishna in the epic story of "The Bhagavad Gītā". Arjuna is horrified by the prospect of battle as he scans the many friends and relatives who ready for war on the other side. Krishna, a mortal manifestation of a supreme being, works diligently to convince Arjuna that he must engage in this battle, that a kingdom has been stolen from its rightful governance, that the battle will be ugly, but it is necessary if justice and a balance are to prevail.

Most of us born into dominant centered identities, through no merit of our own, have earned membership into the power of a kingdom, via race, via gender identity, via physical ability, via citizenship, and through other ways that society determines our social rank. We know, just as Arjuna does, that there is a personal cost to endangering that very membership. We remain silent or disengaged to keep that membership intact.

Warriorship means that we have chosen to step back on to that field, that we are willing to engage that risk, that we are committed to bringing a real balance of justice, vitality, and belonging back into the world for EVERYONE, including ourselves. In other words, we can keep the real world out of our studios and practices, or we can build practices and supports that reflect and embrace it and call for the best in each of us. It is my hope that this book will help serve her work and so many others who are striving to build a society healed through justice and rooted in belonging.

In this process, I recognize the critical call for recognition, attribution, and the proper transmission of yoga practices and its importance. Claudette Evans, my wife, is a yogi, committed to this path and builds this into her yoga and Sanskrit trainings in lessons as I frequently overhear as she teaches remotely, post-COVID style from our living room. She has distilled her lifelong studies into the call for all of us, including myself, to rightly attribute yoga practices and to treat yoga, not as a commodity, but as a sacred practice with history, with roots, and with responsibilities.

It is my hope that 365 Revolutions will reach many eyes and many ears and that it will offer a kind of daily refuge, sanctuary, place for individual and collective reflection, and importantly, a call to action. Let us take up Michelle Johnson's challenge, put Arjuna, the reluctant hero of the Bhagavad Gita, and the many other heroes who choose to do the hard work of revolution and change, into our muscles and bones. The transformation begins here, in the wisdom of our bodies, in the stories that whisper to us, and in a horizon that reveals itself in the early morning in our yoga studios, our bedrooms, our living rooms, and on the streets that beg us to show up and act.

We can do this.
In fact, we must.

ACKNOWLEDGEMENTS

There are so many people to thank but the person that initially comes to mind is my first and always listener, Cyndi Sorrell who was at the other end of the cell phone as I finished each piece and wanted input. Cyndi listened, let me know when the piece hit the mark, when it did not, and when it was close but not quite there. My other reader/listener was Andreta Armstrong, her office across from my space where we work together in the Office of Equity and Human Rights. Andreta is a spiritual being and committed to racial justice — an ideal reader/listener. We would shut her office door, and Andreta would close her eyes as I took five to ten minutes to share a new poem. She celebrated her "favorites" (which regularly changed with the reveal of each new poem) and told me which needed more work to land well. These two Black women, more than anyone, helped me keep my course over the four years it took to write "365 Revolutions".

Each morning my senses are reminded of what true devotion to the path of yoga looks like and sounds like, as my wife, Claudette Evans, begins her day remotely with her "Ocean of Ladies" women across the world who hold Sanskrit and the way of yoga near and dear, and Claudette has been a constant reminder to honor the legacy of a practice that has thousands of years behind it and has always addressed balance and justice before I even considered the idea.

There are many programs and practitioners that I have been honored to know, and the work of Native Strength Revolution stands out as a program that is literally saving lives. Kate Herrera Jenkins runs this training and support program for Indigenous practitioners and Kate generously put me in touch with many yoga teachers in training who are spreading the practices in indigenous spaces across North America. Many of the illustrations you will see in the book are there courtesy of Native Strength Revolution, and at the grace and generosity of the program and students who gave us permission to illustrate their images.

Speaking of illustrations, Lovetta Reyes-Cairo was a profound discovery who was already doing striking line illustrations of yoga poses, and we partnered together to extend the identities of these illustrations and have built a whole new trove of images to center many identities that are often missing from a white centered and mesomorphic body type, norms promoted by the industry. We are very proud to feature Lovetta's work in these pages.

I want to express deep gratitude to Marcella Soto Ramirez, an artist and graphic designer who laid out our smaller paperback prototype, "365 Revolutions: Lunar Cycle". Marcella believed in this project from the very beginning and bolstered the belief it could be something of lasting value. She has moved on to her many other projects, which include using her artistry to draw attention to human rights abuses and injustice in Chile, and we are glad she joined us for the time she did.

This book design has been led by Cleber Rafael de Campos who has taken on a number of passion projects and brought immense imagination, patience, and deep commitment to indigenous textile work, which he introduced in an award-winning book design. We are so fortunate to have Cleber working with us on this project.

Early on, when we were first inviting people to participate in the immersive embodied experience of yoga practice integrated with absorbing poems from the collection, it was the Race and Pedagogy Institute at the University of Puget Sound that invited us to hold a workshop at their immense International Conference, held once every four years. I am fortunate to live in a region where Dr. Dexter Gordon, and Dr. Grace Livingstone have made their home and created a fierce and powerful institute devoted to thinking critically about race, cultivating practices on societal transformation, and acting to eliminate racism. They have made this region fertile ground for projects like my own and the many partners associated with it.

I want to thank Dr. Uchenna Baker for agreeing to share her perspectives around justice and leadership. I first heard her at a day-long Women's Network event at the City of Tacoma and approached her soon after about reviewing the book and sharing the intersections between her work and the themes in "365 Revolutions". She is a truly powerful force, and if you ever have the chance to study with her, you should take it.

One of the sweetest, most tenacious, humane, and creative persons I have ever known is Kaitlyn Bowman who has been the Project Director for 365 Revolutions since the completion of the manuscript and the dream of bringing these words to the world. Both Kait and I share the deep understanding that our work is never done, that we must walk the walk, and Kait has been an ally and inspiration to me while tackling health issues and other challenges that would have defeated a lesser soul.

While I have spent several years writing the book and a couple getting it to print, I think of the truest warriors who put themselves on the line every day to create just spaces in the yoga industry, and Michelle Johnson is the embodiment of true north in that respect. She continues to travel across the country and help us all imagine spaces that are truly centering for Black People, for Indigenous People, for People of Color, for people of Queer and non-binary identity, and for all the people that want to transform the spaces they practice in so that they reflect a

sanctuary for all. Michelle's book, "Skill in Action" is a primer for this work and once again, if you see her anywhere in physical or remote distance, find your way there and learn from her, and learn with her.

Finally, I want to thank the teachers and visionaries, Pamela Higley and Vania Kent-Harber, who founded Samdhana Karana Yoga, which blessed our community for seven years. These were the spaces where "365 Revolutions" came to life, beginning on March 1, 2016, at 5:00 AM as I sat on my mat with a notebook and pen, the full light a few hours ahead, surrounded by a delicious silence that would clear a space for this book. This book, in some sense, is the studio living on into these moments.

I

ADHO MUKHA ŚVĀNĀSANA

DOWNWARD-FACING DOG

21

●······

Invert your body
in
witness
grip the earth
as if
two mounds
of
igneous rock
filled your palms
and hold onto
your crouch.

See the waves
rip through the inlet
like marchers
invading
the middle road.

These are the days
that
blood rushes
to your head,
that the earth
we know
ends
upon our flattened fingertips

and the drop
is swift
flight is not
an option
you have staked
yourself
and what follows
below
cannot be unseen –
this moment of driftwood
laid upon beach stones
like an unbreathing child,
untended,
unprotected
unwelcomed
still.

If you were
a goddess
you would do
well
to bend your knees
gently
so that the war
in your sinews
softens,
so that the palms
of your feet and
mounds of your hands
straddle each line
of the Rio's edge
and your thoracic
forms an arch
so that the desperate visitors
who travel under you
feel a brief shadow,
temporary cover
and a sense
that loathing is transitory,
but shade
is eternal.

You would know
these things,
know that there
must be
some give in you,
that no one
can hold the
qualities of rigid and straight
for long,
that longevity
in nature
bends
and that the borders
between people sense this
and can bear the weight,
absorb the posture
and form a hidden ring
for all that pass.
Begin your practice
here.

· · ● · · · ·

Seven studios
with seven students
sing their opening
to the song waves
of the humpback whale
breaching
suspended in air
in this is the daily miracle,
the possibility
the call
to kinesthetic prayer
the implausible spray
left in its wake,
salt and residue
left behind
evaporating swiftly
on the dented surface
of the hardwood
floors.

There is only so
much
you can understand
with your feet.

Our upright bodies
are blind,
the earth is braille
and we must read our way
into both
the fleet morning
and the longer chapters
of dusk.

The richest among us
lead illiterate,

we follow,
hands at our sides
instead of listening down below
through dips and stones,
loam and knotted soil.

This is the book,
the very first,
and few of us
are reaching.

Each cold plank
is an opening prayer
on a hardwood page
that turns
like an ancient
touchscreen.

This posture,
at full surrender,
will make readers
of us all.

Sing us
into descending
still,
limbs carry
the weight
like a gate
that each of us
must form
not counseled by patience,
but justice,
an earned release
and our loving bones
and those beneath us
have vied to rush
this pledge or settle,

but downward, recanting posture
is
a way.

our calves,
our shoulders,
our backs,
adductors
are all seeking
a way
denied by the sails
of Columbus,
repelled at the
Selma Bridge,
held for questioning
at these terminal entries
we must find an opening
and so we send our limbs,
for ballast
downward,
like the ballad anthem
we have
yet to sing
up from
this earth.

Set to this inversion
between
the night interior
and the slivers of dawn
here I bend,
chin distance
from the farmer soil
forehead parallel
to the carpenter's planks,
the third eye
sensing
the sturdy joists below,
above it
jute
woven into this rumor
fragrance that once dried
along the roads of Bangladesh.

My body is in it,
arched in supplication,
by design
by intention
by accident
by unconscious routine,
it doesn't matter,
the blood in me pushed into service
by gravity,
finds my head
and all of my
ways
are laid low
in union to what
once escaped
my standing senses;
I am affiliated
despite my stated exemptions,
I am implicated
not so far from the fertilizer
or acrid dust
of the downtown sidewalk
I just departed
so let my arms
and head
know this –
some positions are well designed

for rest,
they implore
they gather harvests
of empathy
and outrage
like bounty and whisper

"do something with this"

and what was once
a softer urging
will evolve into a snarl
if I feign deaf,
will invade the nasal path,
will pool like plasma
at the brainstem,
my very architecture
is re-coiled into action
and so
whatever follows,
I must not
end
here.

· · · · · ·●

I steward
these forces
of root
and uprising
in equal love
favoring symmetry
over flight.

I become my own
resolution,
the strong middle
that holds the extremities,
imperfectly suspended,
active
brave,
as my muscles
and bones
were intended
knees bending
toward
whatever comes
and we who practice
are one in this
quivering softly
like strings,
opening chords,
arc of the wave,
neither righteous
nor content
entering this time
in exalted
downward faith.

II

UTTĀNĀSANA

STANDING FORWARD BEND

29

We have no resting
posture for
grief
or its opposite
in vigilance
and so, unsolved,
let your tendons
marry your bones
in the density equality of,
suspended sanctuary
like cranes bending
at the near dark dawn
upright
against the seductions
of collapse,
shaded by the likeness
of wings
working hard on this
elusive collaboration,
a preparation, of sorts,
for the news from Belgium,
Boston, and Dakar
and the many desperate other
iterations.

Our bodies,
unlike our hearts,
are built for ambiguity
and so we dangle here
like shuttering pages,
steadied by a constant spine,
in dialogue with gravity
In this long answer
we have made
of our bodies
this prayer that spurns
the former age
of simple resolution.

Waterfalls require a sturdy frame,
bedrock to support
the plunge of rushing channels
seeking the promise of expanse.

To fold,
is to make passage,
invite opposite forces,
to live upon a
single roiling
way.

The waters in us
are forever wild

but the training
is for the earth,

the sedimentary disciplines
pressed into elegant form.

Make no mistake,
we are charged,
turbulent siblings
of elemental energies
and the body
will have its release,
will take its release

in chaos

or in cause.

· · ● · · · ·

We bend in
anticipation of the fall
promised to brown women
in the package of news
about their sons

like looming deadlines
that battle prayer
for equal time

and call this superstition
or protection

but know that it is necessary,

that we either exhale
this stance

or risk being swallowed
by a random, capricious
god of proxy

who takes his due each day

as if our children
were nothing more
than the suspension
of lottery results
that will crack the heavens
and send torrents
once they are announced.

Call us
women of the storm,
creased in hope
and wary vigilance
gathering ourselves into release
so that we can breathe,
while the rain falls around us,
so that we can build solace
into our days,
divert the winds

and settle into this
fleeting perfection.

Some call this
an inversion
but for us
it is a view just
below our tears

and the earth knows us now,

knows us better than the swift,

erratic sky.

· · · ● · · ·

Call us the next women,
more ready than you think,
spring loaded
just waiting to announce ourselves
and get this world up right.

They call us daughters
and we want to know what you mean by
that?
Whether you are slipping
"obedient"
into the back of your lips
or if you can let
"unbridled"
fly,
not driven, but driving
like the phantom steering columns
we press against our palms
in Saudi
or the elections
we are going to win
everywhere
once we get a hold
of the horizon.

We are not hanging out,
every inch of this waist
is reading
into the world
accounting for what you believe,
and what we know to be possible,
tense in that delicious way
that bodies get just before they make the
big move.

We sing into this
like the harmonies
girls build at their best
and we are going to
solve those viruses,
engineer free lunch logarithms
that feed kids green
in every cafeteria,
spike volleys that split molecules,
build tiny homes for the
desperate legions on our streets
and convince you to see us
in a way that
cannot be managed.

That's how we get bent.

How about you?

· · · · ● · ·

So here I am swinging
on pause nothing forward
left in me, just pendulum
with clock springs on
suspension and my back
is saying
"no"
to momentum.

Do you know what it's like
to be going nowhere…
or the relief at the
bottom of the back
to nothing held
nothing gained?

I swing in no time
to the gentle rock

and my hands
have stopped.

． ． ． ． ．●．

There is this
before the rising
a refuge pact
that will not hold
because the earth is true
but the world complicit
and the body is divided
between the two.

This discipline of resting
and opposing
is earned at the waist
under the writ,
below our tendons,
spine in perfect
symmetrical suspense,
our thighs and bones
in lower prayer.

In an age of
un-waiting
we will ourselves
with prelude
like a cistern
of accumulated listening
moistened cups
soon to be lifted.

There is this,
then,
before the rising.

· · · · · ·•

Gather your secret and plans
in this dandelion field of greens
magnified as you close
the horizontal distances
for the pleasure of ground
a finger length from your gaze,
tuck the clippings
into the quiet pocket
below your waist band
for the sojourn
back up.

Let the lessons
of the African survivors
who found nourishment
where there was none,
who cooked those greens,
foraged at such a dear
and daily price,
let those lessons be the words
of your inversion prayer
as you ready for the rising,
the mantra of the simply this:

"Leave nothing behind."

There is none to waste,
not a single trauma
or a medicine weed,
nor the stinging shame of nonresistance,
bring it all forward
as if every shadow
belonged with the light;
dally swift,

then rise —

all the hidden and translucent

for the journey now

rise.

III

TĀḌĀSANA

MOUNTAIN

36

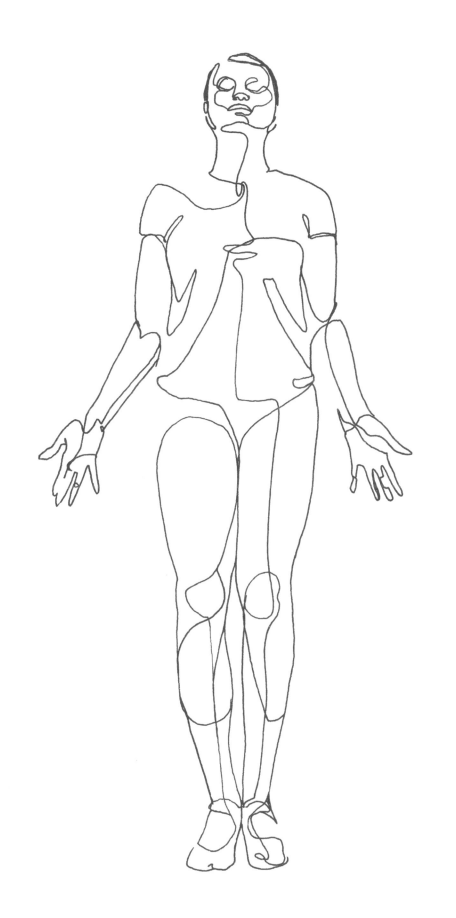

You are not a wall
nor will you
ever be.

You are not
a presentation,
an outlook,
the last word,
an opinion, or a stand.

You are an albatross,
a landing in the Arctic waters
with sheer edges
and sudden drops.

You have split the crust,
arrived
cleaved uneven,
declared your right
to elevation,
cancelled all past debts
collected,
accepted your reason
and the albatross
is 10 miles south,
closing:
you have hidden ledges
and salt water
dripping off your northern edge.

You are no one's obstacle,
a natural homecoming,
unquiet,
far better than smooth,
two paths up
and one destination.

Name yourself.

Roll up in outward
as if your sternum
were the border
of a ledger sheet,
front and back body,
accounted histories contained
along the columns
of your thighs,
summaries displayed
in a simple balance
that makes sense
of the page
unread and waiting.

Now surrender your earth
for the occupied stories
only now escaping
into the open air
on the backs of colored pencils
that choose you
as their medium
that illustrate bold truth
upon the bond
of your fascia
that subdue numbers
in the service of light
and line,
off the reservation,
singing,
shading truth
into every muscle
adorning our
one
precious
soul
at the height

of the original balance.

···•····

We all stand
at the base
of our kingdom
flaunting our parapets
while the work is done
down below.

You are the craftswomen
for the queen,
this day of your rising
and the muscles
work in democracy
as we venerate
the peaks and aspire
to an
occasional summit.

This community of
tendons and bones
must assemble,
led, yes,
but respected
as unified equals
in constancy,
in dialogue,
in audience with our
prescient forehead
elevation
and the way will become clear
in this evolving government
we call
our skin.

・・・●・・・   ・・・・●・・

This is your circumference,
not taking –
but standing –
in power,
nothing to seize,
a strength that
eases up your line
like an accumulation
of voices,
your ancients
are octaves
now
and you are the simultaneous
peak and lower plains,
much more
than the quiet risings
in your legs
alone
and accompanied
by ranges,
one voice amidst
the spinal record,
vertebrae of poise.

So stand,
all of you,
send your sternum
forward
into the good morning,
let the stance
be your petition.

We are the eminence now,
breathing alternatives
to the gerrymandered past,
insistent to the sight line,
power to the margins
along the hum
of respiration,
exquisite landforms
thrumming the circumference
at the grace and distal
of our
upright evolution.

Upon this
enduring body
is a calculation of tears,
storms targeting the face,
sudden crosswinds,
scraping shear,
five centuries of
taking it on the western range
distilled into the simple posture
of being…

and the victory is this –

"I am here."

·····•·

These bones
have been blessed
with the high ground
ever since you took
your standing,
child of the upland
few obstacles
in the daily
sight line
and we could call it this
as many do,
a natural phenomenon
this ascendancy
of ours
won in the clouds
under strict conditions
sipping air like tonic
and certain
we deserve the view.

But we earn
this name
by what scales us,
by alluvial traces
carried on the heel
of a common boot,
by our willing conscription
into the lower plains,
by rugged glacial scars
that end our perfection
in our bellies
despite the music
in our heads.

Take the bottom
with you,
in all its truth and root
begin these days
with a mixture of sediment
and loam
and become the messenger

before the privilege
daring to enlighten
your blank
and blissful
peak.

· · · · · ·●

You stand
this morning
as the visible,
shifts
and risings,
steady on the plain,
asserting witness
to breath and bone,
forward,
meant to matter,
straining for a taste
of the skyline,
contours certain to change
as the salt, snap and
winds
take their due.

All the while
a new formation,
a hidden accumulating
grace
dares its entrance,

fragile,

tenuous,

breaking beyond
at the pace
of how you show
and it will follow
this landform
that never meets the eye
but settles on the shadow range,

a new earth pulsing,

alive in the tectonic chest plates

of the Sherpas
left behind.

IV

UTKAṬĀSANA

CHAIR

44

●·······   ·●······

The view is not a compromise
but a pact with the horizon,
closing in on the
south end stretch
of broken curb, missing sidewalks,
and bullet casings;
on runaways
that would prefer not to trade
sex for lattes and
almond shots
and for fracking discharge
under midnight cover
dumped into the wetland creek.

Settle into the minor ache
of the suspended seat,
drink the water
sink lower
and raise the arms
to heaven
like an apostate
in full surrender
to the doctrine
of the streets.

This acre of floorboard
will not be yours
until you take it,
reside,
test the currents
at cheek barometer,
rest the heal along the pitch,
crouch until the hamstrings thrum,
align with the local grain
and
make a home for yourself here.

··●····   ···●···

This infinite territory
of first nation
must be given its sit down,
it's due,
not the dominant stretch,
but instead coiled supplication,
effort,
the kind of full statured admission
that most of us
were never the first,
that history is beneath our heels,
that an accumulation of daily entitlements
will not make us literate,
that we must extend our fingertips
to heaven
gather all the light,
take our seat
and pull the cover back.

Dig the roots
breach the sky
splay the flutes and
south the thigh
inter inverse
body prayer
twist insole and settle there
Hold these truths at equal cause,
Earthen writ and thermal laws
un-secreted despite the flaws
within these dermal
braille graces.

We strain
for the seat of places
that our standing lives
have yet to go.

· · · · ● · ·

The bones will need this
to thicken within the target body,
this practiced stress,
this lactic,
scorched anointing
that burns away
a weaker house,
solves organic adolescents
with the tested tensile
and compressive resurrection
of a necessary strength
that can outlive
the hostile territories
of these pelting climates.

This is not relaxation
or steady peace,
this is training – that fights back,
that resists,
that invents a fiercer pliancy
in the name
of a survival people
a thickening agent
built tough
within the once innocent target
and it's happening now,
at the crouch of day,
at the seat of power
at the staging site
of the
next revolution.

Think of this now as tribal cohabitation,
the IT bands
joining with the
Iroquois Confederation
to reclaim these lost territories
after a 500-year occupation.

Think of your bones as proxy,
a cooperating force
sent to guarantee
a return
of the original people.

Sit for the waterways
and fishing rights
for an end of the suicide roads
up north and in
Pine Ridge
bring your bands into the fight
like squatters strengthening the perimeter
at a rejuvenated Wounded Knee
and don't rush yourself away,
a reinforcement is rising
up from the depths
of the white earth
and we meet it
at the quiver point,
at the breakdown
at the full surrender.

Steady yourselves
as instruments of the earth
and call upon the waters
in full mischief
to rain on these mats
as if they were forgotten nations
returning,
retrieve what belongs
held now in the
perfect catch of your thighs,
conditioned,
tested,
storm worthy cisterns
and use what you have gathered
in defiant acts of irrigation.

V

PHALAKĀSANA

PLANK

50

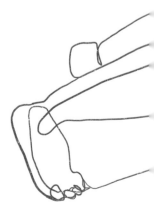

Lift even with the
horizon and carry it
along your back.

Set your
length
into a leveling prayer
and wait
for the surprises
at the deepening strain
of this given latitude
as if your body
was a working revelation,
a number-line of history
where past/present/future
all had equal right
and spoke at the sinews
without taking turns.

There is nothing unsalvageable
when you put your back into it.

I am the grandson
of the railroad tie and rail
gazing level at the lower plain,
even with this labor
and body cost
as I press the smooth
of the spike top,
long since secured
into the muscles of my palms
for memory sake,
for tribute
and for cause.

··●····   ···●···

This is my grandmother's field,
cotton and starch
sailing on the current,
blood and skin,
once a common meal
for the earth,
below my heel
and I am a daughter
in return, prone to faith
hovering at length,
at the scene
at the spot
at the stretch of my fours,
strong like my mothers
but finally, here by choice
and I will take it all in
at the long of the cord
at the small of my back
at the flat of my thumbs
see these lengths I will go
to come

back strong.

My face is
even with the dead
so that there will be
no misunderstanding.

My torso hovers at strain
arms at resistance
listening to the missives
of a whisper nation
since buried
never silent
to we long body excavators
who press into the story

of the low

but never conquered.

Call me
horizontal tall
sleek,
parallel to the earth
I got a back
that takes the distance
for an extended ride,
a mid-body rise
and thighs that dance
oh so steady
to the tongue and groove
sawn and set
to my stationary strut.

Oooh I look good
as if I could hold this
low fly zone
for days
so, go ahead
and gaze
at this victory

I call my skin.

This has been the
instrument of war,
the vantage body
at horizontal arrow,
tactic report
in the tall grass,
low swamp, or
shadowed mountain pass,
the lost view of
a sentence carried
at bullet speed,
the silted grief of
another early mourning.

Now in this blessed
reincarnation
of peaceful terms
we are finely designed for choice,
for life between
these two sustaining arms,
for allies holding up
their separate beauty
in equal formation
for this delicious stretch
of power, ground and force
won hand to hand, at core,
without cover,
without casualty
in the building glory
of this precious
and returning dawn.

· · · · · ·●

In the pores of me
is a map of my
ancestor's migrations
now laid along
my span
etched in latitudinal rivers
across my longitudinal spine,
history is at my back,
I can't see it-
the rail track
I built in inches every day,
the packed and crouching mothers
who survived the voyage
on the hellish schooner,
the dry slats of basket bark
cured along the
banks of the Colorado,
the musket ball
that glanced the rabbit
as dinner sped away,
the northern track to abrogate
a 40 acre lie,
I cannot know these things
by sight
but I am stretched
like an atlas,
feel my muscles ripple
like songs
and these floorboards
are not the end of me,
I am still en route

gaining

a story behind me

with a new passage underway.

VI

BHUJAṄGĀSANA

COBRA

56

●·······

I bend in hopeful arc
at the moment
of my half-life
this clandestine
sapphic smile,
this looping revelation
of a heart
I've kept in hiding;
and now you see me,
at the honest nexus
of my gender,
at full and proud surrender
to the pallet of skin-
this renunciation
of all my previous disembodiment's.

I am not
an apology of nature,
I was meant to rise and
spiral and succeed
and now you see me,
a vision in the tall grass
now you see me
in the age where
camouflage and cover
are condemned
to full decline.

•●•••••

I am not too far from it,
the asphalt court
and diagonal crack,
the perogies boiled at dusk,
the fry bread with two spoons of jam,
Double Dutch
patty cake spit kick pop,
the waning light of
the late night sun
in my window
to help me sing myself
to sleep just after the belt
broke my skin,
my purple hair band
on the bathroom sink
just below my mothers'
outstretched fingers,
the prayer rug worn
at the point of the forehead kiss,
the racial slur that
could not have formed
on my mother's lips,
the pancake batter
that my sister and I
spattered on the grill,
the Billie Holiday somber
sung by my grandmother,
the December that my dads
split up,
the rosemary
I grew in the garden
all by myself,
the mastiff splayed
and salivating on
the good couch,
the long shower,
the very long shower
that I try to take
while my sister
pounded on the door,
the sweet smell
of her hot chocolate
chip cookie breath
when I reached the
baking pan too late,
the garlic frying

on the olive oil breeze,
the rumble of my bedpost
near the elevated track,
the echo of the
empty kitchen
when my father was
still not home at 10,
the schematic
of the slave ship hold laid
on the coffee table
so that my brothers and me
would not forget,
the baseball
that chipped the corner pane
of the French door
laying near the crime scene,
the simple wooden cross
my uncle brought me home
from the Coptic in Jerusalem,
the moose that crossed the backyard
on his late day Sunday walk,
the Buddha on the altar
by the picture of the dead,
none of it is far from where I am,
from where I rise
is where I've been.

• • ● • • • •

We send ourselves
into this new up
rising
leaning with our
all sternum hearts
and unbossed voices;
we, the full throat
reinvention
of one radical body
bent towards justice,
so do not pardon us
as we interrupt,
thrust our moral arc into
your vast and deadened places;
these are the graces
of advanced snakes
in the grass arising
en masse
to even the field.

We are the gods
and goddesses
of torso,
all heart and gut and groin,
living extreme
our belly to the wheel
retracted arms and legs
on account of drag
fleet without foot,
ground dragons
and the sworn enemies
of friction.

We are the allies
of lift
because our bodies demand it
and you'll see us
like lightning bolts
across your hemisphere
and if we are this distillation
of shimming glimmer in flight,
why in the hell
would you ever call us
disabled?

Let me practice
these instincts of
reading the wind
my heart at weathervane rising
above a bunkered nation,
let me join a generation
that chooses to live
o'er ground.

Let us find
each other
and become the advance,
full sternum,
true,
agents
of a longer peace,
earned by interruption
and if ever
there was time
it is now.

••••●•

Send your throats forward
you hidden ground travelers
who sing to nobody listening –
it is the time of your voice.

This box,
this hold,
this chamber moist
will moan no prayers
will speak at pitch,
will lip no conciliations,
and those that governed the five hundred
years,
so accustomed
to hearing their own voices
will acclimate into a new solitude
while the once silent
school this nation
into this justice
of listening.

∙ ∙ ∙ ∙ ∙ ●

This calculation of back and breast
betting on the heart
is not
(in all)
created equal.

There are
those of us
who can risk our day,
guardians at the gate
defending our solitude's perimeters
while we test the limits
of an open source
our chests in the lead

But we of the
fragile second inheritance,
sons, daughters and "they",
have no protected borders,
have never lived
within the case
of that rare constitution,
we the targets of the random,
pervasive and capricious storm,
double gamble our hearts,
stand in those naked fields,
tribute an accumulation
of the innocent dead,
and pray to higher stakes,
send our cause into
bold sternum prayers,
chest to the wind
voice at full throat fixed and
bound by clavicle grace.

We are citizens adjoined,
worthy of this finite and rationed
first inheritance,

and our durable pride
is in fine resilience.

VII

BHARMANĀSANA

TABLE-TOP

65

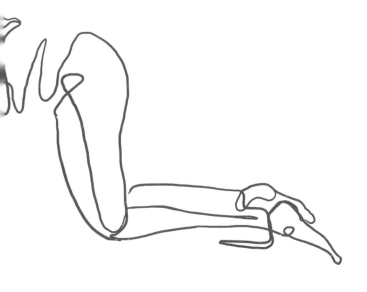

My knees and palms
know this burden
like the double pinch
of gravity,
my torso steady
along the spine
and my back
is for the children,
a lookout, a platform
for the once not possible
and I've learned
to carry the weight,
to give mine
a decent view to level the earth
at the twilight
dangers
of

the crossing.

History has her physics
sending my four corners
down root
as if to say:

  *"this patch is all yours,
  look around and
  don't stray too far".*

But my body knows
the sweet grace
of counter resistance,
I am the champion
of three dimensions
so I rise,
and the sky has my back,
I surge
because my muscles
pull their weight.
I hold up.

Gravity give me

your worst.

I hold up.

··•····

Even the pause
is a discipline
this pride of breaths
to fortify the limbs,
this view
into middle space
this refutation of
the sweet mercy
of collapse,
we are not living
in those times,
no matter what
the devastation
or those lost
in the blast reports
and blinding light;
we are not the generations
that rest for long
we are the ones
that ready our backs
so that the currents
can take up our cause,
race along the
small of our spine
and whisper the next move
to this daunting

millennial sequence.

On the way to freedom
I rested in four –
hands to the three
knees to the one
beats in between
square to the score

I rested in four

I spoke to the plank
and the stone
and the earth
and I sank
and I grew
with my bones
to the mat
my resting was swift
so much testing
to come
hands to the three
and knees to the one
in the flat of my thumbs
the base of my shin
the back flat and even
the tilt of my chin
are the recitative
of the postures ahead
of the lift and lilt
of the wane
and the ebb.
I am still.
I am led.
I am still.
I am led.

They've been
promising me
this patch
and my palms
are trembling
at the corners,
knees are bone down
in constant prayer
and my back
is squaring up
against the sky.

I've got this,
and my limbs know it,
won't settle
for an easy walk away,
rally into the low horizon
of torsal covenant
and seal this sacred earth
beneath me
so that no one
ever again
can treat me

like
open ground.

· · · · ·●·   · · · · · ·●

The backs of mornings   Between the good earth
are held by fours   and the tree line I serve,
at the early rise,   set my spine plumb
steady and even   to the current,
solitary muscles   listen to the order of the day
enjoined in   and strum stretch the flexor
common cause   to ring in the strong
daily architects   that my back has become,
of this leveling,   my muscles are the steady
a warrior   carillon of my
array of light and   ancestor's song
fire collectors,   woven like tensile strands
charging,   of acoustic wheat
storing solar courage.   and I am the lattice,
at the base   durable,
of these scapular wings   particle,
stretched in tabular unison   pulse and wave
one people   pulled together
rehearsing,   with my core
compressive strength   ascending.
in place of words,
equal to the weight.

Better.

VIII

BĀLĀSANA

CHILD'S POSE

70

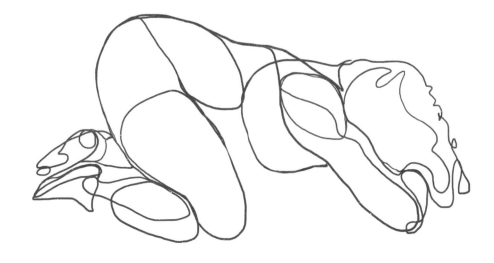

●······   ·●·····

Lord let me rest
against the bosom
of this nation that
keeps heaving me
back up on my feet.

Let me live and stretch
and lay my forehead down
into a tranquil pool
and just not think a while.

I got a little ocean in my hands
and I rolled it clean
along the rumbling territories
and I got to believe
that even history
has to take a breath
every once in a while
so here I am supplicating myself
for a little drink of blue
for my hands on the water
and the rest I'm gonna take.

The secrets of the revolution
are caught between my eyebrows
and my knees
at a pausal interdiction
just below the torso;
in other words,
there are some of us
recharging up in here
and even earth forms
coddle natural conspiracies
just beneath the common plank.

So don't get too comfortable
with my modified supine,
I'm coiling at the moment
but when I do unwind,
well,
it's gonna to be me
and the bones
and the soil,
allies in the third migration
at a liberated stretch step,
rapid and fair,

but that's for next week,
the day after prayer.

Kneel me next to my youth
where I remember my forehead
on the sweet and level earth,
where soil blotted my skin
like a smudging benediction
where all of us must, had to lay low
or else get in dusty trouble
in the knee scuffed dusk.

And while we all trudged
double slow
across the door jamb
into the un-wild
of the split plank plain
the world waiting
has not been equal since
nor held those
low ground promises high
but I kneel because I remember
the common truth,
it grounds deep
into the beauty of my browner skin
and my patella shin
and I know that these truths
must be kept,
not just evident,
so I gather in the low space
where the child
hears her song.

We spread our backs
in purpose to the stars
and at cause
with the sun
because someone's
got to be the book
and bond,

each day

yet to be written.

Constellations in
perpetual dictation
using our latissimus
as their writ
and we are renewed
as morning pages
unruled and waiting—

Each body receives
its calligraphy dancing east/west outward
from our celestial spines
word within us
where once
there was none.

· · · · ● · ·

I think the turtle dreams.
Sand.
Sinking.
Just enough
to tickle his shell.

I can make
my body into this.

He gets quiet

Inside the dark.

His breath is tiny
like two grains.
No one sees him.
He's waiting.

I can make
my body into this.

. . . . . ●.

I breathe
the floorboard grain
into morning
my hands flat
against the palms
of the ones
who laid maple at purpose
and culled
and planted
and planed

and no corporate distance
can erase the oil
from those fingertips

just a whisper
below my head;
they live
under the varnished rings

and I owe something
to toil
to perfected
locking seams,

to craft
and these
men and women
and underage conscripted

are worthy
of the center square
of my voice at my rise

are listening
along the threads
of my sleeve.

This one exquisite
kneeling exhalation –

tinder and witness

spark and fuel

a breath
to carry the story
upward

give word
to the underlay
and the flat work
and stitch

through the cuff
and the binding

the tongue
and the joist

give word to the underlay,
give word,

give voice.

· · · · · ·●

In solitude
where light need not answer,
time is generous
sorting ancestors
and songs beneath
the inverted convex
of our portal prayers.

We are at once
a communion,
alone
and at infinite company,
seven generations behind
and seven forward,
listening to the
instant wisdom
of them all.

Take counsel
with these people,
sip each breath
like a separate voice
and gather yourself
like a village
then rise,
child to womyn/man
loving brave
within the intersections.

IX

PARIGHĀSANA

GATE

79

●······

At the end of
the occupied bridgeway
you will find yourself
free
torso marching
toward
the solar dawn
your dorsal array
more than equal
to gravity,
released from the swift
and bone batons,
the gaggle of fists
and sanctioned chokeholds
that have blocked our centuries
right of ways
as the cost of resistance
at the first
and second legs
of the span.

The walk means
more than
dodging and
enduring
the measured blows,
the walk belongs now
to the things we carry
and what seeps
between the
pinch of our shoulders
and the resolution
of the spine.

So here we are –
better than the gauntlet's hammer
stronger than the
cuffing grip,
breaking free.

Clear.

One knee down
in supplication
by choice now.

This is your
body at
stretch liberation
and you've earned
these minutes,
the swallow of sun,
the overture of a
full throated sky
singing along your fingertips
welcoming the swinging
tendon doors wide
like a solid breeze
into your waiting bones
both an archway
and an open border
just beyond
the whistling hinges.

My hidden body
rises,
lung strong lobes
reaching past the former boundaries
of my compressed voice,
a refutation,
a practice
into the air
and I am present
at the opening
a living halo
wrapped around these
gathering inhalations.

Our bodies
and vertical bones
are wind instruments,
in fanfare to cause
with a single elbow
lifted like a trumpet
to the sun
sending word
and ascending song.

I take a knee,
to this patch of earth
not to own —
but with inviolate curve,
one side body
repurposed as
shade and shield
and we will need
legions of the same
to cover acres in days,
underground springs
and aquifers,
elder cairns
and August Prairie Sage.

Let this arc
be a message—
long,
bent toward the
god of small things
and the water's share
my arm in
holy camber
with so much ground
to cover
and no contingency
but the grace
of our limbs.

· · · ● · · ·   · · · · ● · ·

Children like
my eye to eye,
my brow to bridge
my on the level –
in other words
no one seeks
the looking down upon
for too long
so come back
to the "low"
take a knee
and make like
a double rainbow
let the kindred
be the light bending
at the river
with your eyes at elevation
and no one
at the high ground.

Limbs and rafter
ground and truss
palm of felt stretched
across the span
along my left and
my right is betrothed
to a footer array –
the shelter we build
begins here –
as those in homeless wonder,
as the jungle thickens,
as the sewage
finds no filters,
we are the body
of a new imagination,
lengthened,
staked,
swinging open
toward the empty acres
that deserve a better plan,
we are the carpenters
rough and finished
we are the architects
and neighbors
who refuse
the restrictive covenants
of the era passing
we are the design
and welcoming
the single knee
the home for all
better than a posture –

home.

· · · · · ● ·

What you must know
is what
I leave behind:
the songs
of the original tongue,
the angled light
along my former pitch
of longitude,
the bitter root
and home spice,
the mud and monsoon,
the sharpened knuckle
at the predawn door,
the splinters left behind,
the phantom loam
that the knee remembers,
the impossible loft
of the baker's wind
from the corner pan,
the jawbone white
of the empty plate
and the crumple
of the burlap
with my daughter listening –
but one cup of rice
to stretch for days,
the sparrow skim at mist,
the sweet in the common air
that has no equal, I
put this all into an anchor limb
while the converse
becomes my fingertips,
bold and blind
strange molecules
and measures
just beyond
my grasp.

· · · · · · ●

I'm over – heel at the lean
ulna on the loop
"Bring me your tired" –
the stack and the score
melanin magnificent,
eleven tenths citizen,
amped without Ritalin
I am all over this nation
and my body means
where it's staying,
don't fence or lock it –
I'm wide.
I got language for days.
With the memory bank
here in the knee
I cap that
and trap that free
we are not
the former position,
don't sit well,
the way I reach
and hang
is all I need
to tell.

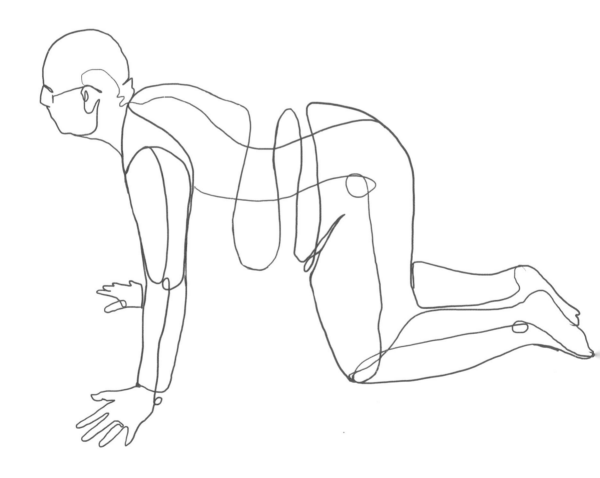

X

BIḌĀLĀSANA /
MĀRJĀRĪYĀSANA

CAT / COW

85

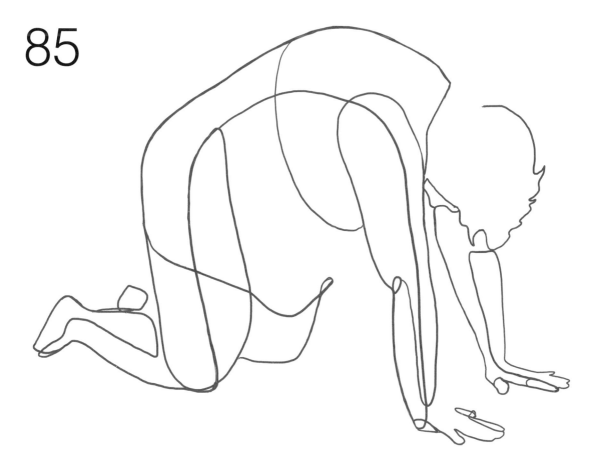

●· · · · · ·

(Cow)
Join me
as we live
in the round,
bellies proud
and out,
enlisted lovers
of spectacular inhalation,
sphere of the transverse
abdominal
stomach pristine,
unfettered by a
flatter reasoning
we go big and
we go strong
like deities
of the jocular dimension,
all craw,
unobstructed
swallowing our
daily molecules
like champions,
breath to spare
orbit warriors
of the
tongue and air.

Let us love
in our natural bodies
and global bellies
and quell our corners
in declaration
of the coming swell:

  *"I will not hold myself in.
  I will not."*

Show and tell.

.•·····

(Cat)
Rise like archways
and make way
for the waters,
troubled and swift
back reaching
for a little taste of sun
and sometimes
there is none,
the run is froth
the skies cast
and the roil
feels like reckoning.

Our fingers
hold back nothing.

We are living
in a time
of torrents
once underground
now barreling
along our riverbanks,
anger swells,
nations chasing rain
and sure it comes,
our position neither
gauntlet or dam-
we are the four points
of its edges
joined at earth dimensions,
leading,
leading,
leading
the raging current
until it has spent itself
in vain,
our spines in exhalation
at the bottom of the skies,
count your vertebrae
with vaulted femur
and rise.

· · ● · · · ·

(Cow)
You will find my voice
pumping at the back of my breast plate,
outspoken
unbossed
totem of the living,
emissary to the horizon
beating
bigger than words
and you got
no choice
but to hear a chest
at full volume,
treble bass and blast,
no whispers now,
one muscle
singing
through the cages.

・・・●・・・

(Cat)
Every body
get behind
some sanctuary.
I make room
and put my
back into it
while my compass mates
go to the mat
in
formation —
no silence of friends
we are a movement
holding the center
high—
always
a space
for you.

Call us the people
with a spine.

. . . . ● . .

(Cow)
We of
the pregnancy
are about
to give birth
to a majority:
olive,
black and
brown
unbound
by the dual gender
clause,
pink of a
deeper melanin
mentality,
womb enders
of the age of
minority,
new entrants
at the pelvic floor
just waiting
for an introduction.

Bellies to the earth –
listen to our children,
more than harbingers,
better than prayers,
breath of the sages –

a nation in delivery.

· · · · ·•·

(Cat)
The past
is behind me
but ever present
like an outdoor practice
played
among the night constellations,
ancient stars
along my unsuspecting spine.

I need not name this
or know it
because light has its way,
makes its imprint
like a needle map
along the
dorsal meridians.

And if my fascia
is the willing page
what will I read
into my
surrounding atmosphere?
How will I meet
the colonized earth
below my knees,
how will I reconcile
my palms
to this soil tilled
by indentured fingers,
how will I brace
for the bass trill
of those who yearn
for our guttural beginnings
and would trade an orchestra
for brutal blast of bass?

The past is
neither consolation
nor revelation
but it must be
reckoned and
so I raise my back,
read the light
and reject
the common
linear wisdom.

Be.
Be in two places.
Be in two places
at
once.

· · · · · ·•

(Cow)
Look fierce —
full horizon
no drag,
lock in,
convex attitude
belly down
vision forth.
This spread of plains,
these prairies
and riverbeds
all of the alluvial
peripherals
need this
trust of sight
this survey flight
each day
each morning
each hover and swift
full on steward
no drift
pilot
hold position
just below
the fingertip
lift every eye
in a troth
of equity to earth
cut the current
report and engage
in ocular defense
witness and
protect
full speed
engage.

DAṆḌĀYAMAṆA BHARMANĀSANA

SUNBIRD POSE (BALANCING TABLE)

94

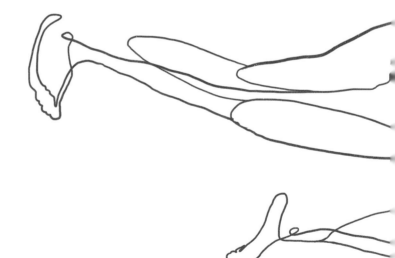

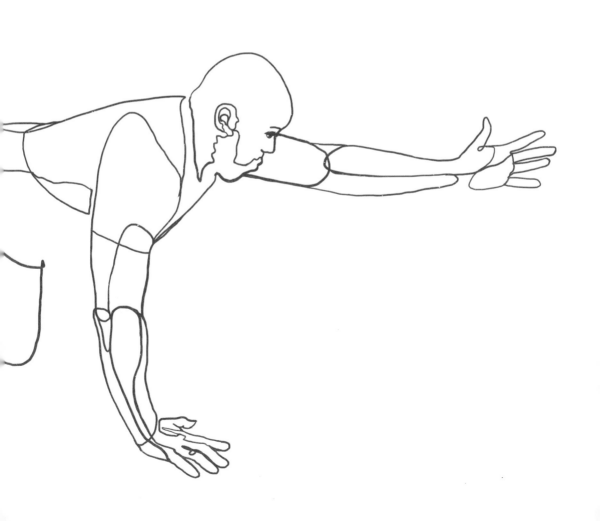

We who synchronize
in ground
and air
send one half
into the unknown,
warrior limbs
clearing a common path,
vigilant sweep back —
toward the strange histories
behind us
until the swinging stops
and we steady
into witness
forward toward the winds
fingerprints reading the
constant eddies
of a just barometer
we have yet to grip
or receive
and those
at balance
are the anchor limbs,
ballast to my temporal spine,
accurate and still —
in my palm
and its pulse
at the bend.

Let me activate
this fiercer symmetry
negotiate to pliancy taut
launch my ends
and spend this day
beyond my reach.

You think you
know me
by means of
where I begin,
the evidence,
the side I take
the nascent and
visible intersection
at my start,
but I have a
side waiting
a yearning reach
that waits its turn
at the first
and in its time
I become my own author
this body you see now —
how I choose to define
and finish
a wiser pose
informed by the
first but
insisting on a center
of my making
glory at the sweet diagonal
a second life pulsing
at my fingertips
and you suppose my lead
but I define my end
and at my breath —
such wonders!

··•····

I live amongst
the ways
of this side –
share the incidental
and selective histories
settle into our
common preliminaries
and wait for the
next instruction.

But my alliance
of bones
in the muscle keeps,
know the ache
of this un-extended
absence,
the deep involuntary reach,
the investigation
that goes unsettled
and
I am no stranger
to my better impulses
my ankles
and wrists –
twin students
in common cause,
disobedient spies
just flexing
for a scrape
against the veil
beyond my heel
and palm and
once this side yields
another is waiting,
a prima facia
of calculus
and kingdoms
a dig
and a root,
my opposite fingers
at odds
with silence
and we will know
the balance –
there is no
secret
that the
body cannot find.

· · · ● · · ·

This is the skin
of roads traveled,
worn,
ready
brown durable
migration highways or salinated
billow sea,
skim and crest,
south to north
east to west
first leg and willing arm
of this fresh emancipation.

No one title
binds my
slick surfaces,
the causeways
my edges and stops
I am my own declaration –
no need
for your pen.

In a half millennial
land
of holders
I have none
and the second leg
is coming,

no meander
center route,
torso out
song along
my shins wrists
unbound,
post itinerant,
at long last length
and
at
home.

· · · · ● · ·

Let this now
be the
asana
of franchise,
durable and
clean line
tensile limbs
defining my reach
and boundaries,
no crooked paths,
no trace
of gerrymander –
a spine
at simple truth
unbent
and boldly cast.

This is my
get between
my "excuse me?"
my "what did you
just say to the
Somali couple
speaking in their
own tongue?"
This is my
dance of interruption
my silence no more
my
"you shall not pass
the slurs beyond your
tongue
into open space"
my fresh life
of dinnertime
interruptions
when you thought
your ugly was safe
this is me extending
from 26B to 1A
across the aisle
in such a way
that a man
can speak in Arabic
without getting
kicked off
the plane.
I am in this now,
have activated
my spine
and when my right reach
gets tired
my left one
is just fine.

Blessed is the practice
that straddles hemispheres,
elegant lines
that cross diasporas
fingertip and sole

The best of us
live in two,
not built
for simplified
contractions
but for horizons
available
to those
of a rigorous
and fortified spine –
hallow this kind
of muscle
courage
symmetry of bilingual voice,
tendon and patella
singing stretched
like string –
multiple longitude destinations
along the
vertebral stack,
a body both
home and
visitor
that
by this practice
is fit
for peace.

XII

VĪRABHADRĀSANA (VARIATION)

HIGH / CRESCENT LUNGE

100

●·······

It comes to this –
600 million bones,
tired of secrets,
find a gesture,
yours,
ocean possessed,
tidal fight,
taking your lats
like apostles
sweeping the spine
into pliancy
curved into
an antonym
of desolation into
a hard song
a call
and obligatory response
blasting from
your fingertips
a continent
rising from the ulnas,
singing Woloff, and
Chamba,
Mbundu,
and Igbo
with nations
still waiting
for the muscle's way
in,
and a powering crest
about to reach
its
second leg.

This rises
from my original belly
full shout
while my fingers
stretch into
the blessings
of empty space,
no rectangle pinch
of plastic braille,
no tap and binge,
no spirit,
powder
leaf or
needle to
taint my palms,
just this inheritance
of a natural root,
this absence
of my common twitch,
this first person story
unscrolled
clavicle to wrist –
rough and guts
and wits and grace
thrusted prints
outflexed
in the act
of composing.

I am not
the single blade
nor its proliferation
to civilized trim;
I am the kale shoot,
fennel,
crooked pepper
and golden beet;
I rise in wild plots,
insurrections
of collard bloom —
food,
real food,
for the redlined,
casted off,
an act of harvest
spreading,
a market
at every curb,
uncolonized volunteers,
soon to live and
fight by this
new belly wisdom,
wealth to fill
the empty bowl
sunflowers
swaying
like a sovereign
flag.

· · · ● · · ·

There are prayers
to put your back into
shelves to stock
cans of pintos
to stack
the row of
breakfast burritos
that are heavier
than they look,
carrots to pull
before the sun
fully rises,
bread pans to lift
at 4:38,
flower baskets
that need the water
of your extra reach
lunch counters to scrub
twice before
you flick the "open" switch,
rice to heave
in a burlap sweep,
the arc of triumph
as the bag lands high, Jonagolds
that answer
to the gentle tug,
a toddler lifted
to the
lukewarm tub,
crayons to place
on the tiny
table rounds,
blankets to fold
at the ready worn fringes,
coil the straps
and square the bolsters,
salt the lots
for the predawn spinners,
Nana steadied
on her
loo-bound walker,
a double arm of chum
scattered off the bow,
mounds of coffee berries
to scoop and sort,
the quilt tucked

just along
the hospital fold,
the old cottons
sorted
into three
color piles
for the coming loads,
the frozen snow
chiseled beneath
the ice chunks
just outside
the tavern door,
the banana bowl
placed before the Buddha,
The Sunday Times
rubber banded in plastic bags
packed in back
of the old Camaro
on a Sunday run,
the tiny cups
of wine filled
with the Zinfandel
10 minutes
in advance of service,
the casket rolled off
it's casters
toward the view
platform,
the shingles dragged
in bags toward
the ladder,
Nana gently
lowered into
the leather seat
of her wheelchair;
there are prayers
we hold in common
and by these errands
we toughen
into fine sinew –
fiber and divinity,
woven allies of
our once
and ever
reach.

· · · · • · ·

To serve the
grounds horizon,
get low

there are people
waiting for a
measured scoop
of kindness
for the supplications
of a strong
and humble torso
for listeners of a
concave dimension
who gather frets
like rain
and keep them
safe
in the crook
of the ulna,
find your place
on the broken plains
hidden underpasses
and broad daylight
shadows and
listen for the pain,
hold your frame
and welcome
these troubled migrations,
send your forearms
upward and carry
these desolate
moist
fallow
spaces.

Let this be
my gender clarion,
built for steady,
certain,
rooted
outlasting the
tyranny
of the analog age.

I am
what I say
I am
what I know
within this harbor
along the
adductors,
I am a living declaration,
self-named
in perfect balance
pulling earth
toward my voice.

I name
myself.
Now
and after.

Consider these advantages –
the fluency
of my skin to air,
my mastery of pressure
and it's microscopic changes,
the sonar
of this voice
with the map
of abiding surfaces,
the fact
that every city,
every street
and stair
and kitchen,
coffee shop
and carpet
surrenders
it's secret score
to me,
that I am the audience
to earth
and decibels
and my ear canals
accumulate these riches
in an audible universe
that never goes
silent.

I raise my arms
to a moon
I cannot see
but the tides
and the tugs
and the pulls
are within me
and this muscle organ
instrument I've become
is the home
and haven
to such grand
and subtle
elemental
forces.

XIII

VĪRĀSANA

HERO POSE

108

● · · · · · ·

*To the survivors and
descendants of the
Japanese American
concentration camps*

I sit upon
two soles,
my own – at rest
and one in waiting,
my knees
the bone top
messengers.

Listen earth
to the lives they took –
the farm and porch
and bento box
and walk to school
and Evergreen and
grocery store

and packed us for a journey
into dust

and listen now
to the balance:

my return,
my seat upon the space
I deserve
my upright frame,
grace and witness,
my stubborn kneel
upon these varnished
Douglas timbers
that my fathers set.

My ankles flex in deference
to the cause

and I am one –
othered
and
resilient

I am one.

There are those
who will keep
watch
under shadows,
rising
each morning
to send
a warming
breath into
the margins
and it's
not so much
that
the dark
declines,
but
that in
witness,
a new forming.

To set
in
these places,
to inhalate
it's warnings
to kneel once
each day,
is
to be aligned,
and oh such
cause and courage
to swell
from this
horizon
perch,
oh such cause
and courage
such tendered
cause and
courage.

Mat — my Pacific,
knees —
my volcano's source,
I am
every bone
the island,
cool, once
the liquid brim
in the scaled rock,
formed,
an upright
resolution
of warrior
at
the water's edge.

I cannot
be owned,
this spine
is my statement
rising like resistance
with
just a little
give.

This gaze
begins
in embers,
in this throat
a fire song.

I cannot be owned.

I cannot be owned.

· · · ● · · ·

The dawn
belongs to the lock
and
the sliding gate,
the wall
has got my back
and still
I sit for light.

I am full squint
through the
steel grate
trying to keep
my ears clean
and teach
my spine
to sing,
hidden
like silent night
but proud
like I train
myself to do.

This is my freedom
and it's small
but I am stronger
than the ways
they bend me
and
if I believe,
it's in scattered slats
of sky,
recycled,
yes,
but
those particles
reach me,
despite the odds
they make it
through the narrow
where my pupils
can find them
at the secret pass.
You can hear
the whisper
between us –
Iris into light
despite
the plexiglass.

· · · · ● · ·

At the end
of the superior promise,
fallen,
I come
to my knees,
upright and abandoned
like the strips
and storefronts
for lease and renewal
on the middle
of Main.

The steel, the coal,
oil and lumber,
plain English,
the pension and
the rights
of grazing –
a tumbling corrosion
of prayers
that disintegrate
at the milepost
of the
county seat.

The original trust
is broken –
the guarantees of color;
call it "eggshell",
brittle and false,
crumbling,
so as I sit
this front
gives way
to my truer
flesh
and I am
at the
tender mercies
of the
crosswinds,
practicing this
blended new alignment
with former strangers
who have outlasted
five centuries of
sleight and consolation,
independent and awake
at
the dawn of
the second watch.

......•.

I am collecting witness
at the bone narrow
settling back
into the harrow
on the heels
of winter
in the
forehead courage
of spring and
naming a literacy –
violations taken
upon me (and my kind)
as if we
were more thing
then breath.

Hear me
I am not,
nor will I ever
be
your silence;
I do not acquiesce,
I discern
I parse
I sift
at this pause
and gather the
compacted pain
like crystals
in my palms.

This is the science
and art
of it and
I am at the knees
of testimony
greater than equal
to the yawn
of the
event horizon
And by this story
I did not fall in.

I am a teller,
my spine
is pen and
we are not
the ones
to be
unwritten.

We are not
the ones –
and you will
know this
upon our rising.

• • • • • •●

I sit
in an act
of separation
my ankle settles
into the
sovereign ground
and my hands
fall into the serenity
of my knees.

As I breathe,
freely now,
I'm not your object
or your confessor.

No appeasing smile,
My face is at rest,
and this distance,
as I lean
into my heels,
is intentional.

The work is
ahead
and I leave you
to your own facing.

XIV

UṢṬRĀSANA

CAMEL

116

●······

Let my sternum
rise like
this new
century
and petition
the mesosphere
for equal time
with the stars.

My breath is light,
my chest still believes
in promises
and gravity
is a weak adversary
to my
pulmonary will.

We were born
into this fable,
or migrated
to this myth
and now
my blood
won't settle
until the sky
meets my cage
and by this kiss
by this kiss
do ordain
my rightful
elevation.

This lifting body
is not
a coalition,
a confederation,
a collective
or a free
association;
I am a concentration,
strength from my practiced
and unknown limbs
of my cousins
and the similar
families
I bring from
my core.

I am not
these parts
I am indivisible
and in this
moment
uncolonized,
child of a
fiercer God,
citizen,
initiate
but not a
democracy.

I tilt into
this aspect,
vaulted thoracic prayer,
closing circuit
of shin
and hand thunder
at the plains
of Quetzalcoatl,
Durga surging along
the flesh
of the ilium,
Dotson' Sa,
eyes lifted,
clavicle at pre-flight.

I am pure invocation,
power,
a lucid Being
at this
naming place.

I am born
on the mat
and I enter
with
no caution.

I am set,
organic vessel,
bearings for altitude,
this xiphoid
now
my protein
compass,
angled toward
velocity
and escape friction,
a prophecy
of stars ahead –
and even with
these outward
calibrations
I must
earn my way
to the sentience
that awaits.

We are not
entitled
to this firmament,
must discipline
our way into
membership
by this reaching
strength which is
the best of us,
and the vaunting
depth
of our humility.

Join.
Depart the
era of conquest.
We will not
reign supreme,
and if we
are to travel –
leave
that fiction behind.

I posture
in this time
of heavy forces
that favor
ground and gravity
fist and hand.

But this
land
of sternum,
this territory
of my breast
resist the supplications;
I am greater than,
an elevation,
reflecting sun
and alpine will and
500 colonized
years of compression
are no match
for my tall and
settled strength.

The length
of my lineage
began in moltency
and lead
to the searching
eminence of my
new and
ancient heart
and we are
forming ranges,
a future of uprisings,
an interruption,
a contradiction
that rises
like natural law
to reverse
the physics
to bring the mountain
to raise
this earth.

· · · · ·●·

My dream body
is the one
that knows
where the water is
and holds it for me
until I
can wake up.

· · · · · ·●

My gender
is a revelation,
a miracle,
a backwards plunge
into blind
and bracing
waters.

Full shiver,
I am alive –
shaking off
the pronouns
that hung from
me
like oversized
cottons.

Peeling these
sopping remnants
back, I am sleek
and good,
all across
my front,
dripping dry,
rising through
the open air
this is my
undiscovered body
and I name myself – this fierce
unguessing frame,
I name and
let it be known
that I,
once lost,
have now completed
this first and
most essential
posture.

XV

ANĀHATĀSANA

MELTING
HEART / PUPPY

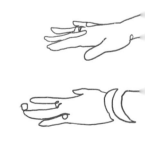

●······

I live atop
the tiny plots of
missing gratitudes
and I know
my earth
needs gestures,
my forehead as
an offering
of faith,
tobacco along
the blades,
a libation poured
from the height
of my palm,
tender lips
parted toward
the dirt
of my prayers
and then,

the waiting.

·●·····

I am old
in this hating,
rallied like tossing
stones
in an ever world
of windows
struck skin and bone
and broken –
only more of this
waiting
in the throes
of the anger prophets
with paper crowns
and I am tired
of the

against

in all of this,
of the following,
of the crack
and rubble
I've become.

So pull my heart
to dust,
ready me at
the knee
and I will listen
for another way –
at the low
of the soil,
the cool
of my cheek
the bottom spaces
where
no one
is king.

The earth
of the
migrant step,
of the tilling fields
of the
anti-bellum
escape
of the cucumber
and potato spread
of the
Jonagold orchards
and the twist
of the stem
arid carpet
of the spindle
and thorn at the Crossing,
the terrible crossing,
must be learned
at the height
of the chin
on the Intimate eye
of the abnegate pose
that makes an
enemy
of distance.

The second age
of the parent
is a revelation,
best done
off our feet
in the place
of our softening
postures where
we can love you,
far away from the
high ground
where we can roll
into the
magnificent
earth
behind
your eyes
where the judgments
of our height
gives way to the
throat and trill
of this song
of yours
this song of yours
this
perfect
song.

· · · ·•· ·

Thoracic rise
along the
kingdom of
my skin,
my body
begins
in the Nile Valley
at the throat of
Kush
call my chin Ta-seti,
and my tongue
the fertile plains
of that
original city.

The practiced eye
above my brow
saw the sphere,
knew earth
at once
as a circular dimension,
seven thousand
years of science
and civility
stretch
along my spine
and I know
the astronomy
is behind me.
I reached
the Americas
by those triple
currents
I paid the pyramids
forward
and now
my body returns
to my rightly
discovered
geometry,

I am as strong
as my numbers
swiftly serving power
to my base
fingers spread
like mapping
constellations.

I am the frame
of the founder

and I am home.

. . . . . • .

. . . . . . •

The pectoral plane
and the flight
of this earth
do not ally
endlessly,
our chest
angles
for wide
and durable
spaces,
for sabbatical
followed by
the necessity
of return
for the inevitability
of the rising and sweet,

so troubled
winds.

The earth
is my accomplice
and she never
wanders,
my pulse
is her confidence
and she keeps
my worship
like precious secrets,
double metronomes
of flesh and loam,
syncopated liberty
and as I believe
so does she
haven me
in grounded trust
and sheltered intimacy
and from this
clay
I forever
form
my church.

XVI

MĀLĀSANA

GARLAND

128

●······

Mine
have waited
for a
just standing
longer
than we can
remember,
endured the
peltings
of target kind,
advanced at cost,
and used
the oil of
our tears
to grease
our hips
into a suspended
descent –
hovering, healing,
breathing
along the
lower plains.

Don't mark this
as our retreat
but make it one
of many coilings,
the practices
of lower strength
to suit a swift
and certain
rising.

．●・・・・・

I'm always
near it,
the bumps
and pits
and cracking ramps,
the mean curves
and steep pitches
the grates
and the rumble
the double muscle
pump
of my arms
to the wheel
when the incline
is rough,
the downhill
and strain back,
the hairpins
that I clock
around the
conference chair,
the blessed smooth
of a good pave,
the beauty
of a lawn
and it's rock
and muddy threat,
the poetry
in the bricks,
the toxic slick
that makes
an enemy
of traction,
the boardwalk
that juts
into the Delta,
and the heron,
the single

heron

that
meets
me halfway.

I'm always
near it and
I live
what you build
and what you won't.
and I sit here
with one demand
re-formed
in prayer—
make me
your supreme architect
and thus retire
your once
and lesser
god.

Accomplice
the waters
get low
below the
pleasure of your hips
and listen
for the conspiracies
of protection.

This life
we are straddling
takes to the underground
to the dark
and buried
springs
and big space
has nothing to do
with survival.

These are private
matters
and no halfway
will settle it –
so lower lower
you're heading
to the underworld

lower.

Let us,
oh sisters,
gather in fours
and name us
the quadriceps
femoris.

Know that
we built
the fires,
sustained
the pots
of
our invention,
pinched the thyme,
carved the ladles
and kept the council
of our mothers.

Call this a
practice of equals –
that we greet
our children
and morning fennel
with similar zest,
that we are the
keepers of the flame,
when our hamstrings
burn
it is ancient,
that our glutes
are
kindling
and our heels
strike twice.

Let us stoke
long
as women do
and make our
plans
and keep our
eye to eye
in these secret
and familiar
spaces.

· · · · ● · ·

· · · · · ● ·

I end this –
the screens
and offers
appetites
and blasted volume,
an empire
of boost
and deepest treble,
pushed to
bass assault —
I end this,
accede,
errand my spine
to plummet,
stop short
and hold
the void –
these are
the silences
of spirit that
happen here
in the
down
below
this is
the empty full,
my daily finish
in this
season
of resistance.

At the feet —
where the chains
are hidden,
I join a nation
of obstructed
vision
and send my body
down –
low
along the shards
and links
and driven spikes,
plumb upon
the ankles
of this altered
Liberty,
tight into
the pitch.

． ． ． ． ． ．●

One.

XVII

UTKAṬA KOṆĀSANA

GODDESS

137

●‧‧‧‧‧‧   ‧●‧‧‧‧‧

Mine is a body
built for the
facing –
the eddy sea,
the wind
in bracing,
the mighty clock
of the sun
and the
nets waiting,
the un-conceded
ground,
the verdant tracks
of Papatūānuku
just behind me,
the width
of my chest,
the revenant littoral
resting there,
the shoal
of my groin
and it's warning –
I am built
for this,
and you
advancing,
swallowing spans –

I am
built
for this.

Let us
remember
the body
of my people
who live
with hands
up,
breathing
an impossible
endurance,
untenable,
a calculation
into the gravity
of exhaustion.

Let us remember
the body of my people
who live
with hands up
breathing
an impossible endurance,
goddess rising
through their shins,
surging through the blades,
and on into
the elbow's knife –
let our bodies
be our warning,
blaze
the martial postures,
barge the stolen boundaries
and carry
past
fatigue.

This is my body,
unaltered,
blemished,
scarred boldly,
muscles along the bone,
like onions scattering
my earth, a
strength at right angles,
width --
harvest and defense –
a natural owner
despite their deed,
power through
the raking tines,
my feet
at mortal grip,
not a pose
but a stance,
stamina and
harvest
first confidant
of the seed, the
ground trusts me and
I've earned it
down by Elegba,
a planting
at the crossroads,
this is my body origin,
an interruption
of invaders,
tilled-
omni-indigenous
to everywhere
and anywhere I
stand.

· · · • · ·

You made me run
from this feminine
even longer
than my
first remembered
sun,
and I am
always
just ahead
gargling
at gasps
before I need
to move again –
until today,
young man
of the special sun,
which I have always
been.

I stop
and let the woman
rest,
rest hard
on this ground,
no less
have I ever been
though you
had convinced me –
no less.

I am not effeminate
am imminently man
in this way
that rages you
but I am
not running.
I am permanent
and partial
to this
taking ground
a miracle symmetrical,
body making peace
on this
sediment and kindness
on this making
on the
taking ground.

· · · · · ● ·

Attend.
No fast twitch.
No shift.
Attend
to this body waiting
to the sister lost
to the cost
of her silence
and the stories
we dare not say.

Attend to the debts
and the burdens
of the few who rise,
to the cellular stress,
to the self-neglect
as a consequence
of this tribal saving.

Attend.
Stay put.

Let the heels deny
a thousand concessions
for the good
of this mat,
and the boards beneath
and the concrete base
and the earth below
and the rich
deserving
reason
that we have
already
earned our right
to attend.

Attend.

· · · · · · ●

My body
is the
first
constitution,
self-governed,
evolving,
immutable,
protected —
woman
as
The Word
and I shall not be
breached or bargained
or bow
to lesser law.

I am the standing
of supreme,
inviolate,
a tome
of majesty
and curve
and breath
of primacy.

I defend myself.

It has come to this.

I defend myself.

XVIII

ĀRŚVA ŪRDHVA HASTĀSANA

SIDE BEND IN MOUNTAIN

142

●······

Think of my body
as
music at rest.

I am not
the efficiencies
of
my desk
or the morning
razors edge.

I am bent,
a swoop,
a tilting branch,
scent of fruit
on my
fingertips
an intermission
of my former vigilance.

And if we would
make
a world
where limbs
like mine
were safe
to ponder
I would rest
here
longer.

·•·····

I enter pliant,
flexible,
bamboo ready,
built for high wind,
a living cultivation
of my ancestors'
guile.

I know this soil,
the storms
that sweep it's top
and the memories
lodged
tough
in my
stem.

I am the
wending strength
at the end
of all this
and mine
have outlived
the origins and
calamities
of an
un-graced
founding.

Behold
the arc
of my spine,
bending next,
tough and unbroken
feeding the loam –
visible in a
victory
of root
in the rich
and blackened
underground.

．．●．．．．

I've lived
the postures
of the front
and back
absorbed the
dual economies
of a promise forward
and it's common set
behind,
known these
corridors
along my narrow
living strip,
inhabited this
scarcity –
and I choose
a life
among the laterals,
a bounty
of friends
and strangers
yawning
in limbs and tangles
and chastened
syncopation
at clamorous play.

My body seeks
the literacy
of my former
peripherals
awakening
to the
marvels,
tilts
and splays
beside me,
to the casual stretch
and determined
reach,
to the common
task
and flirt
of this nimble
village,
to the side
of me,
dauntless venture –
to the
side
of me.

···•···

Settle into witness,
take a position,
one side
or the other
in orchard
silence.

You are
not
the only
to see
these things
to know
certain histories
at the blurring
edge of the
nail
to hear
a distinct
unfolding
deep
within the quiet
rustle
still along the stand,
unguessing.

Lean in confirmation
to what you know
and sing
unto the light
without the fiction
of straightening –
one truth
twice bent.

····•··

At once
a canopy,
my torso
sadness
protected
by the wisdom
of my arm,
dangling in siesta,
so fleet these
pulmonary winds,
so sweet
and hard
my grief
in the
suspension.

But it is strength
to plan
your own
haven,
to get
beneath,
to sob
into the luxury
of time,
self-given,
and by these
waters,
rest.

• • • • •●•

What if
my shift
is subtle?
Not the tendon
drama
of the lunge
nor the twist
and sight
reversal
that brings
such changes –
what if the new way
begins
off my
common line –
if one tilt latitude
distance
belongs to another
scene
and I
am one waist bend
away
from a richer
shadow
or a
bolder
light?

What if I leave
these physics
untested
settle into
safer
deprivations
and live the ways
of the straight
and upright?

My spine
cannot love
in the field
of these calculations
my eyes
will not leave
the vertebrae
behind
I am the arc
and it's discovery
the light
calling,
the flicker
and it's tinge,
the unanticipated,
the path
along it's
taking
the math
and it's intention.

What if my
shift
is subtle?

· · · · · ·●

Mine have taken
and owned
their spaces
as a common
practice,
splayed
and lunged
and rarely listened,
limbs
claiming territory
once pristine,
pulsed familiar
to the
anthems
of content
and distilled
ourselves
into
giddy
interruptions.

So just this once,
this second life,
let my
side body
answer
in a reach
so strange,
rooted here at
my
lonesome heels
silent fascia
trained
toward wisdom,
a learning pose,
a visitor,
a quiet lean
to the mysteries
I have never known
in the places
that were never mine
to own.

XIX

UTTHITA TRIKOṆĀSANA

TRIANGLE

150

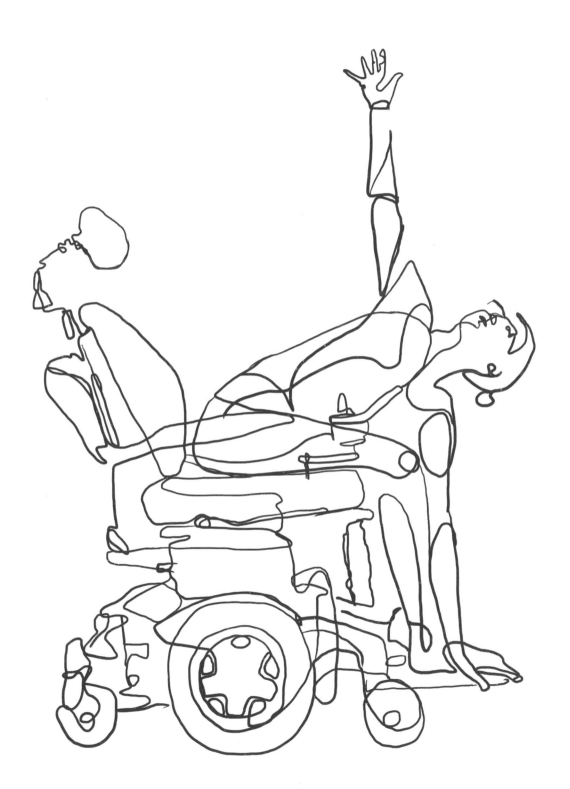

●······

The open story
is below
my heels and my
fingers
reach for
the prairie top
and the
page below
for the women
and children
lost
to the slugs
and blades,
to the thing
they called
destiny,
the manifest,
a frenzy,
a seizure
organized
over centuries
and the best
in me
digs,
despite the ache
for the blood
in the
ground;
it's secrets
and this airing
I find,
filling
in the base
of my
throat.

·●·····

Hand to the dirt
thumb to
the sky
big open
chest and
arm at my thigh,
triangle telegraph
wireless spy,
the palm at
my ankle
closes the circuit,
I got this
third eye
and I know
how to
work it.

Work it
work it
tell me
the truth
I'm going
to find out,
indestructible youth
that I am
to my waist
and the end
of my spine,
blade of the plow
and fork
of the tine,
mine are the fingers
that dig
to the root
and stretch
from my bones
for the high
hanging fruit,
call them the stars
or the words
in the wind
I got the yang
covered
and I'm coming
for yin.

Let my body
form no apology,
seek the fiercer
histories
of so many
stories underground,
seek sun
and all its science,
ecology,
the firmament,
survival
in this fragile
place
of life,
these are the priorities
to place
into the memory
of the stance
I take
and my eyes
are on the swallow,
the way
of wing
and light,
my eye
is on
the feather
lifted shoulder
unconfined.

I set myself
true plumb,
limb pitched
like a
survey pole,
opposite arm
raised in witness
to the
original ones
and in this
discover
my
first allegiance.

I am not above
the story
nor is it beneath me.

I am level,
living this moment
of truth,
rattled
and serene,
breathing hard
breaking ground
shaking off
the silences
like dust.

. . . . ● . .

I start here
at the low, quiet, tapped to sand,
soil,
weathered ship lap,
grave near
the Southern gate,
rubble quarry
covered bones,
polished slate
ruptured stone
from the
sacred sweat,
prayer mat
now worn thin,
weeded lot
on the sharecrop
plains,
cedar floor
at the longhouse,
tobacco-stained curb cut,
I start low
like this
and know my
lift,
long arm
rising
like an upstroke
splash of cyan,
like fancy finger tut,
like a cool gel
on a bare stage,
like the page
I type
terse and clean,
this palm speaks
as if my stretch
was an involuntary reflex,
ground to air,
caterwauling keen,
against
the common silences.
I trap deep
and crack air
and I'm
calling it
art.

Our mystery
is bone to earth,
it cannot
be solved
through sky alone,
troubles the loam
and bedrock
of every
conquering myth,
shakes off
our adopted
loathing
and finds instead
this exquisite
point of root.

We are the perfection
of our original skin,
breathe well
through the
wider nasal passages,
sing full
along our
melanin octaves
and in this
the heavens
rise up
through the buried
molecules high
into the hand
and then
we join,
only then
we join
children in this
waking family
of infinite elevation.

And on this
my seventh day,
I am bent,
collecting,
uncommon
riches
at my heel,
rail spikes
and skin,
hidden flasks
from the migrant's hand,
bloodied peg
of the Sundance
thong,
wooden cross
from the Coptic palm,
a slurry
of tomatillo seed,
a
concentration camp tag
dangling
on
a string
of cranes,
this practice
of gathering,
ankle high –
panoramas
at
such humble
elevation.

XX

VĪRABHADRĀSANA I

WARRIOR I

156

This
is the
standing ground
of my century
and
I'm taking it.
Call me the
advance,
the look of a people
after the
extinction fails,
the rib cage
in this time
of stout expansion.

I am not
going back,
nor will my heels
let me,
center of the mat –
no margins,
sky as my witness –
this is my
standing ground.

Women in all
the
we,
in once
such
isolated no
standing,
un-placed,
Center less
cornered
no step
forward –
step forward
in all we,
in lunge
unlocked
knee,
enrise
one
together
no only
in our arms,
the once
no
space, full
and
we
taking
we taking our place
that's the what
and that's the
we
that's coming.

If you have wondered now when I raise my arms no sequence or submission something is rising long before I get there and call it the length I go or the mercy or the grace or the welcome shadow I am the age and its privilege at this no decision not a skill but something lived into fickle never earned just once is worth this lifetime.

· · · ● · · ·

My mind makes
voices
like hail
from the perfect sky
covering most
of the quiet ground,
recurring storms
and falling bodies
that scrape my bones,
scar the stapes
of my inner ear
and I feel each
collision
in my life
without shelter.

I am the shelter

I am the quiet ground
sibling to the eye,
encircled by this chaos
and
I do not
answer.

My mind makes voices.

I do not answer.

· · · · ● · ·

These are not
your horizontal days
of rest,
of supplication
of biding
and submission.

We are the vertical
nation
once quiet,
settling
for the
view
and it's obstructions,
settled no
more.

We, the provocation
send our bodies
to petition
to count
the millions
deprived
of health
and all
its privileges,
assert our
standing,
insist upon
this commonwealth –
decency.

And we rise
against
the seated
and their neglect,
we insist
upon a unified
care
that holds us
all as evident,
as tended,
as the once
and future
body.

We stand in
warrior.

One.

• • • • •●•

This religion
of mine
has no book,
enrises
like a story
still telling
favors the
tongue
of spine
narrates down
the calcium highway
of limb and bone,
disdains
the lag of time
and forms a new,
untested
earth.

I stand in
this fragile
ecology
against your
certain God
and what I know
is that
the same God
does not side
with you,
bends toward
our common
lung
and
I am curious.

If there
is sIn,
it is in your
crush for cancellations
hurled at the pace
of falling stars,
neither wish
nor wonder
to these ends.

Yet,
in faith
my arms
aloft
I say:
"This world begins".

· · · · · ·●

Remember me
as this,
single arrow
tautly strung
about to sing
my way through
a thousand constellations.

In these final
meanders
as my spine
bows
and bones in
awkward
spiral fix,
I am not
the anguish
of body's end.

I am this –
a perfection
of line and arc,
an epic statement
of intention,
a manifested
call of arms,
unisons ringing
through the
augment
of my fingertips,
heels notched
and tendons
ready
this is the
yes
of my crown
against
mortality
and all
its mirages.

Let fly.

I continue.

XXI

VĪRABHADRĀSANA II

WARRIOR II

164

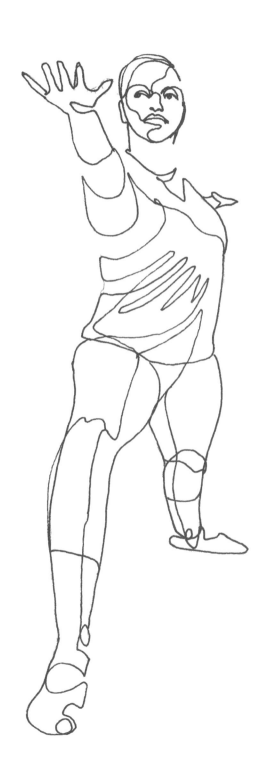

●······

I got no
use
for blind spots,
hands reset
and I'm livin'
in the 360.

Yeah,
it's got
beauty,
but this
is a survival
spread
and a tribute
to the dead
who didn't
know what was
comin'.

Raised among
the kindred,
eye on the light we know the opposite have our own back cuz trouble is the price of living here.

I take
the line of
setting it
right, got my
rock base strong,
Long in the vision
with a touch of wary
and two full fingertips
of cause.

That's the
double side
of the daily story
and I'm
stickin' to it.

· ● · · · · ·

Water
river well and
farm,
tiny plots and
humble patches,
this is the
standing ground.

These are the
silenced places
beneath our soles,
The eminent domain,
and the realm
of the missing,
and we will not
deny them witness.

Raise arms to
rally a fresh
alignment
hold this
liminal advance
long enough,
just long enough
to flesh our strength,
trouble the vacancies;
and these waters
and plots
and patches were
never yours to take and
we are
not your silences,
but it's inverse
embodiment
from this throat forward
mark the opening
from this throat
forward.

I've been living
like an arrow
since the days
of my un-sheltering,
longing for the
One Direction –
out,

There is no other.

I've been
taking my body back
one untangled limb,
then another
found my inviolate set
and now my fingers
sharpen north
shoulders firm
in the shelf
of my horizon
and heels
draw the bow.

Sing the one word
sing survivor sing –

Out.

They are never far –
just beyond
the fingertip horizon
treading the
yellow tiles
of the primary cafeteria-
these conscripted
to the compulsory
weekend fast,
Dannie in the salmon knit
who lays down the
two cans of albacore
upon the moving belt
once a week
and nothing more,
the girl
who sleeps below
the corrugated
overhang
when all the
school buses are
gone,
Ester
in Kiambu
who piles the
brown stacks of banana wilt
for burning,
the pillaged garbage can
and the homeless man
smoking the nub
nearby
outside my yoga studio –
all by the flat of my thumb,
A perfect constellation
of wont.

And what of me?
How shall I set myself
to this savage plane?

· · · •· ·

You have no idea
how alone
this gets –
how quick my friends
of one thousand days
and dinner tables,
a Thursday Bible
and barbecue Sunday
can traitor me
into the garbage call.

Where I tremble
at this
stand,
my scalp does not
smell sweet,
sweats ammonia,
muscle scream
fast twitch
sprint
while somehow
I stay at
lunge root.

I rose
in the land
of othering,
of smile violence
of such a vile naming,
of this
and hidden flags
of a diner mug
smashed into
an immigrant skull
for the language crimes
of a refugee
and these violations
took their toll on
my neutrality,
until my shoulders
unwilfully spread
like the shelf of Christ
all arms and
heaving chest
and I
could not stop
my body
from pointing yes
to simple decency.

But you have
no idea
how alone
this gets,
how the heartland
stops beating
in one
arrhythmic sweep
and
I am but my fingertips
praying –
faith
with nothing
but my heels
to read the magnets
and hope
my precious mettle
points me north.

· · · · ·●·

My body
named itself
long before
the courage,
core insisted –
ineluctable
as if nature
knew the way
and girded me
for range
and distance.

I live my answer
and its daily threats,
the taunt and jeer,
the drive-by
and muscle shirts,
the hiss
on the public wind
and the gritted bliss
of my revelation
ground into the
toughened plantar
wisdom
of those
of us
who left the war
and found
our root.

· · · · · ·●

You tell me
to fall in line
but my gender
rejects that
flat dimension
toward the forces
of an endless sphere,
and hard
as you judge
my outline
your vowels sing false
you have no name
for me
lost in the mirage
of double wisps of
binary smoke
as my winds
pick up and I
resume the loam
that you've forsaken
dig my heels
into the silences
and sink my two spirits
into ankle time.

I have no center –
don't look for it –
don't look for me –
in your notebooks,
your locker passes
your name plates
and Bible verses.

I am older
than all that
and you are not
yet ready
for this encounter.

XXII

ARDHA CANDRĀSANA

HALF MOON

173

●······   ·●·····

In my preparations for the half-dawn,   Curious,
steadied by the veil   when I invert
and the slowly   the hierarchies
giving lIght,   of standing
my back is beautiful   and dare
knows the way of the night,   to see along
holds me up   this new folding,
at these common wanings   the once high
and height holds   seem, well,
no quarter here,   curious.
these are not the sights
of standing   So much forgetting
but of the low   amongst the elevated –
horizon   so little root
and by my steady—   to feed the topiary
such plains and wonder!   and such fleeting
                                              contact
                                              in this life of plenty
                                              and all
                                              its deprivations.

                                              I tilt toward
                                              the lighted balance,
                                              ghost averse,
                                              gripping my shin
                                              like blood family,
                                              set strange
                                              and plumb
                                              along the sips
                                              of horizon,
                                              breathing even
                                              and hidden
                                              by the posture

                                              of the perfect blind.

Play where you stand
not in this life
so upright
serious
when there is
ground to tumble,
thrilling ankle totters,
big down
bend up
flat back tricks
landings to stick
and sites to see
from the way below.

Get so tired of the
un-smile
and un-high yourself,
un-high yourself,
into a body dare

or two.

I am the
skin of the
waking dream,
a twilight petition
of my ancestors
in cistern and sanctum
formations
square to the oats
and wind
and I have past life
promises,
rising to my scapula tilts,
to keep,
breath to sing
from the lungs
of my family
and reveries of justice
to drop
into my shins.

I am the lunar sail
at full spread,
the tide's intermediary
and those who surrendered
their spinal pleats
un-crease
and unfurl
into bold
and unresolved
animal geometries
that twine
our pleadings
forward into the waiting mats
and tender heels
of this time.

· · · ● · ·

Upon my witness
there is no old ground;
the many clever fictions
surrender to my wrist
and palm,
to my freestanding arch
and covenant heel, to the
many inverted myths which
cannot keep their balance
when I supplicate
low.

These tracks are new
the dew is fresh,
and so I enter,
close distance
with a black, attestant soil,
bend bright
into a lunar trust
and reap my vantage
of the understory
just this side
of the
near dark dawn.

I cannot love
an earth
beyond my hand
and so
I bend to it,
listen to the hum,
smooth,
gravel and grain
of my low,
requited strum.

I am
infatuated with you –
at the post of each finger
and the
river of my thumb.

I am the needy one.

The journey
of the
10,000 miles
ends
at the base of my palm
at the bend
of my waist
at the sudden taste
of safe ground,
not in the credible distance,
but the impossibility
of my deliverance
and I am the waters,
un-dammed
at the weeping edge
of this known world,
ready
to salt the earth
and not so shall,
but already,
overcome.

XXIII

VIPARĪTA VĪRABHADRĀSANA

REVERSE WARRIOR

178

●······ ·●·····

What if the pitch
and breadth
of my sternum horizon
was founder
to the minded blade
and
swifted arc
of my sword?

The ground up knows
and signals
the sun—
This land was built –
these cities
these columns,
piazzas,
cathedrals,
plantation rows,
treasury foundations
and temples
of the word;
were tethered
not by
the mighty,
but the hands
of the indentured
plain,
the unwilling,
death knowing
proud
and angry weary
who put their
rage
into their craft
and now my hands
send the stories
back to say:

   "No more secrets.
   Credit my people
   and pay the due.
   take your generations
   to set the fields
   in balance
   but now is the
   sky to know
   not in the names
   you give us
   but in the people
   shall be named."

··●····   ···●···

Crack the viscid
of my
side body earth
and sing
to the tip of my
macular reach—
I love this one.
Blessed by the territories
of my skin
sanctioned
by the truth
of my throat
and twi-shin
stubborn end;
I love

this one. ·

My spine
is my
theology,
my faith,
my democracy,
the parabolas witness,
a quiver
to the open air,
to the business
of arcs and
all that free
in this age
of maximum blocks
and time lock
steel.

I believe
in the honesty
of my reach
in the natural curve
of light
in the vertebral sweep
of my holy bones
that sing *"citizen"*
past this flat
and decimated
horizon.

I advance
in elder –
tempered
tip to base,
a reaching victory
of balance
spectrum of cause
from ground
to air, inner pose
taut,
neither scream
nor whisper,
an extended interjection
of reason –
an evolution to power
is what I am,
change to the molecules
surrounding,
troubling the waters,
an elemental force
in it's
second homecoming
arm aloft
at my return.

I advance
and name
this

"elder"

My body seeks
its own resurrection
despite my daily burials
in binges
of eternal sleep.

I am the agent
of numbing passed
through these
many generations
to my waiting cells
into this strange
and awful
obedience.

but there are
deeper voices
singing through
my fingers
resistance
in my shins
and so I stand,
light as my witness,
a poor student
of conditioned surrender.

I stand in this pose
of a daily miracle
and bend
in the angles of
interstitial re-fraction
and once
and yet believe
my eyes
once and yet
believe my eyes.

. . . . . . ●

I share the life
of the once brown
dead
on this continent
of humiliations
and many days
I live stories
added to their own
concertedly etched
onto my crowded
latissimus pages
and they accumulate
and I send them
rising through
the writ of this
back body
toward the balm
of
a listener.

Still,
you allies
and innocents,
teams of the supposed,
self-claimed
good,
standing
in similar poses aside,
collect your precious confusions
cradle all the comforts
of your darkness
and all its benefits and
give your answer
of destitution:
"I must be imagining".

500 years
of this—
practiced
and shined
to luster
and so
much of me
is dead to you
and will remain,
until you emulate
more than
the outward posture
until you rise
with me
until you hear
the littered bones,
until you sink into
this
and only then
with my breath
at your ear
born of sob
and gasp
under the weight
and liberated
reach of
a new alignment,
will you know
what it means
to stand in
warrior.

XXIV

UTTHITA PĀRŚVAKOṆĀSANA

EXTENDED SIDE ANGLE

185

●······   ·●·····

I will not   I shake my
soldier these   limbs
new wars   to steady my wait
and be   and set low
your violence;   into
I will train   an invitation,
my angles smooth   a living way –
so that the rains   still forming –
roll along me,   an acute yearning
and the storm's outcome   perfected as if
forms no stagnancies here.   I were
                                     the first call,
I am the instruments   and my back
of a greater   was a
reaching   divine cartography.
side body
to the sun   We are the children
at swift tilt —   surpassing the comforts
an evolution   of the upright
from the age   and perpendicular minutes –
of demagogues   not the straight
and we are meant   and shortest lines
for better things.   but the sublime diagonals
                                     the ascendant
I am not   and crooked routes of
your army.
                                     a change is coming.

This is me
making shade
with my side body umbrella,
twice as strong
and twice as cool
as the super genius
hot grownups taking
it on the head
for no
good
reason.

I am
a flag
of rivers
at the dissipation
of once
and former nations,
a devotion of ground
to light,
no side to favor
yet I give each
in turn,
my ribs
are the rain ways
and if I anthem
it is in the
key of sluice,
a catchment song
of this grounded standing
and this is how
a bigger universe flutters —
through me,
and angle ready
for the truth
in all its winding.

If you take
my line
as beauty
stand aside
and join.

I cure myself
of the distractions
that keep me
from living
the truth of this ground.

If I am low
there is a reason –
I am listening
holding confidence
gathering the decencies
of my line is eschewing
the bleak accumulations
of the preferenced dream.

I am
the better story
and you will see me –
buds o'er reached
but never done.

My faith
is in my heels
below the knee,
the crouch
in the gently
burning crook
of the holy writ –
Torah
Bible, Gita, and Koran.

I started here
like living embers
so why should
I not warm
to the callings
of my gender
and the way
I choose to love.

Great faith,
grow to meet me,
chosen home
invite me in

as I am

invite me
in.

· · · · · ·●

End that question
Forever
at the back
of my shins,
at the balls
and toes
of my rooting
along my psoas
and it's hard-earned opening,
end the question-
I am from here-
I stretch across decades
in this posture
I call
"citizen",
in this reach
of railroad ties,
blackberries,
sugarcane and cotton,
my hands and feet earned
that title long ago,
and we are present tense,
building,
always building,
despite the question
and all those
customary exclusions,
animating a thousand
side body streets,
we are the pulse,
the builders,
end your outdated question
which does not emerge
from innocence.

I am from here.
The ground
is my nation.

I am from here.

XXV

UTTHĀN PRISTHĀSANA

LIZARD

190

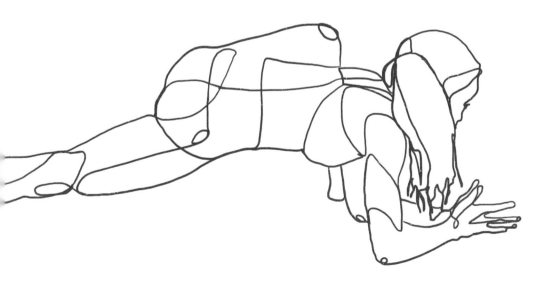

●・・・・・・   ・●・・・・・

I welcome
my new affiliation
of no apology in the low space,
nothing now
between my breastbone
and the warrior
ground.
I am heart
and groin
traveling the increments,
the millimeter dust,
the crusted roots
and their fertile compounds,
advancing
on the belly
of my skin,
all in,
civilian refutation
whole obliteration
of the once
and never
three fifths.
I am
the harbinger
and
if you miss me
also the trailing
leader
and I
bring word.

I bring word.

We,
the unspoken
bring our throats
into cherishment,
a pact of the
un-secreted
who make
this ground
our common
revelation
and we are tight
to our word
and the strength
all fours
bring.

Call us
the contradictions
of silence,
the truth
above a whisper,
the reclamation
of this
survival body
and we are
life now,
in all the swift
and
startling appearances,
apprentices of light,
masters of showing,
bold on earth
and warming.

Let us gather
below the fences
in the under country
where we of
one hundred
shades of
ground
finally
make our plans.

Long are the
big house treacheries
that pitted us
to our unnecessary
solitudes
and deep
are the grains
we swallowed
throughout
the choking seasons.

But this cool below
is a place
for words,
for the stories
we left behind,
for the sobbing
currency still with
us in
a cloud-break
of tactics to
muddy
the Estates.

Stay with me
and unblock
your throats
while we
settle this.

Listen
to the song
of the lowering
sun
for those
who know
that night
will come.

The pitch will rise
the light will fall
my limbs
to stall
in darkness.

Within that amniotic space
my shin and heel
flex and trace
the ground I'm leaving

the void and grace

are simultaneous here.

····•··   ·····•·

Hear the water,   Answer the waters.
the crystal hum
and keen, the split scream
the silting, sifting filter
thrum,
the toxic collisions
and mourning plume,
the chlorinated fanfares
and sedimentation
score.

The music
of this earth now
is rarely pure
and the rivers
will reach –
decibels of the spring
one chain
below us,
ancient songs
swift and
unstacking
to be learned
on our bellies
and loved
in every smooth
and
broken scale.

· · · · · ·●

I am the appearance,
a breed so silent
that we are forgotten
along the sills
and thresholds
of the center house,
blood bound cool,
generations of wait and see,
stealing sun,
a reconnaissance gathering
along the gated courtyards
and it's cast-iron,
jagged welcoming.

Call us by our plurals –
an infiltration,
a discovery,
once deferred,
thieves of avarice
in all it's
crooked light,
taking the heat
of the Terran star
and claiming it
our own.
Call us the breach
and arrival,
the agility,
the molting hide,
crest
and ancient crown.

Call us the revolution.

XXVI

ARDHA
HANUMANĀSANA

HALF
HANUMANĀSANA

197

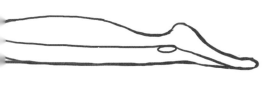

●······

This is the first prayer
of the new body,
the preparation,
a taste
of the impossible span,
the end
of anti-bellum
and all its
antecedents
the beginning
of the many micro
tears we call
a stretch,
the bold sting
of my leg bottoms,
this will hurt
well into
another age
and all my
contractions
spasm toward
a fight
they will
not win.

Not the
supple body
of our mythic angels

but the
untuned strings
seizing
as we have a go
at this
again,
reset
at the half point,
pull the story pen
into our forward heel
and lay our
mat
onto
this page.

Our body strives
for what is unwritten
for the outstretched
promises,
for the
unannexed new land
of a founding
without coercions,
and the truth
of our fierce
and full extension.

Call mine
and my pose
the original name.
I am ahead
of you
and your borders
came after.

What you name
presumption
is my deep
and lasting ease.

I cancel your geography.

I am the original name.

I was born
into one body
but I am
making a new one.

Set deep
within a lower
fluency
I denounce the gravity
you imposed
rise from my own,
and stack up brave
to cross
the span.

I'm pausing
on a patch
of destiny
unkept because
I need some time to think.

My papa
and his,
knew some promises.
but this land
is skipping me
and my sons,
and tons and tons and tons
of others
so, someone needs
to tell me –
which
way do I stretch?

Who do I reach
when all the
blaming's done?
What do
my muscles
know
that they are
telling me?
What kind
of new way
will my crooked ankles
point?

I got to align
myself
with different company
and figure
this thing out.

This extended prayer
into the house
of my raising,
it's aisles and pews,
upon the mat
and blessed niche,
upward toward the bimah,
tight along the lighted sage
and wisping embers,
becomes my body,
mantra of the living distillation,
my tendons taut
petition song,

  "Let us all
  Let us all
  Let us in."

Banish all your scarcities.

  "Let us all
  Let us all
  Let us in."

And so
I set my niche.

Before my leap
is my unknowing,
with just a fleeting sense
that I am progeny to wind,
that my generations
fought the ocean
and wilderness
to dig ourselves in,
that I posed
to many fictions
and my mythic knee
never sought the strand.

And with this end
comes the preparation,
the heel in the sand
the tense
before the twitch,

the caution,

to the wind.

XXVII

PARIVṚTTA PĀRŚVA KOṆĀSANA

REVOLVED SIDE ANGLE

202

●· · · · · ·   · ●· · · · ·

My turn,
I'm on
one side of
this,
never going back
shadow on
my
prayer
pressed into
my
palms,
a mineral rage,
cooling.

Twist a way
back
to the coil
of my sheath
and
my breath
long since
holding,
I am nested
in
a thigh of
discontent
and yet I'm breathing
the tomes
and
hollerings
of unconditional
equivalence,
plea,
demand
equal wages
of this core
constitution
I am at
peace
with a
war for
full recognition
and you will receive
this side of me
before you
see
the other.

I pose in
"deliver me
from my
daily walk"
at the foot
of the bed
just before the
out the door
and into
the blood corridors
lottery map
of the
don't
choose me.

Don't choose me
on the
two-mile
gravel strip,
unlit
facing headlight
plunge,
or the random
pop
crackle
snap
and gone –
just gone
wrong turn.

After they
close
another dozen
my learning
starts here
not at the
school bell
but before
the dawn
with a prayer
that on this
day
somehow
I'll see it.

We of the chronic,
strong on
Monday
but gone
on another
not of our choosing
of random immune
wrath
with no reason,
rally our persistence
to stack our
daily outcome
into the square
of our palms
as if this
were
a work of will
but our hands
cannot close
tight enough
to stop
the seeping,
the inexplicable fatigue,
the missing strength
on this day,
the hair unwashed
because
we cannot lift it
the un-sustaining breath
and unrelenting sigh
we are cloaked,
the desultory
stricken
of
a working age.

Our torsos
turn
toward the prayer
on the clock,
to the next number
to the following day
and if
we cannot meet
it
will you believe us?

· · · · ● · ·

I turn
to the Presence
at my vanguard
an expanse
beneath me
that somehow
I've traveled,
a discipline
of stature
and mystic council.

I am these things,
so says my heel
I am these things
by flexion
and my
mastering palms,
an effort of
miracle
in fierce
and tender
progress,
heavens graft,
the undergird
and rising.

Young man,
I can hold
my history
in the echoes
of my shins
but you
best not be
waiting
because
the cities
of my youth
have ended.

If we were
All the movement
knuckle,
knee and song,

You are
another
all pace
with no
apology,
a constellation
of elbows,
the cool
and
the stone.

My long muscles
know
the physical
migrations
of the
won't look back

of the
north and distant

of the
ragweed roads

and the
no rent signs

and this place
that I've found
needs
a new migration

a heel plant
and learning

a demand in place

a fierce
and firm meniscus

a spill of light
between my
threaded fingers

One swallow
forward

into that
loving

breach.

XXVIII

HANUMĀNĀSANA

POSE DEDICATED TO HANUMĀN

208

●······

These are the
wonders
of my
legacy body,
the miracle
of my
spring
and vault,
survivor
of the blooded tears
and all its trails,
the migratory skim
above the whip
and cotton,
my launch and
measured splay
into the southern groves
and northern orchards,
my landing
into three generations
at the assembly line
before the closing,
my stand
to end
the plan of the
poisoned river,

the will
of my spine
that outlasted
Joe Turner
and his
many kin.

This is me
at the glory
of my
adductors stretch,
ten branches
to the current breath,
a blinking
outcome
alive within these
troubled plains.

This is my gain
a launch
on behalf of the
croppers
and the casualties
a leap into
the heart
of these matters
no longer
a preparation –

aloft.

•●•••••

This is a
practice
against
a clutter
of objects,
a declaration
of space
while the frantic empire
screams it's play
on infinite channels
to the
consumed
and always listening.

I am the
living ingredients
now,
tension at
both
my poles,
a forced
integrity,
full lift for survival,
thigh blades
troubling
the waters,
clear of the
coastal disintegrations
and on into
the interior
migration
of a dangerous
and verdant
New World.

····•···

You will recognize
the
initiates
by the ease of
their impossible
suspension,
by the way
they carry
and hold
the span
by the tensile
strings
leased along
their bridging bones
by the opposites
unable to breach
the integrity
of their heels
and vaunting
spread.

They are the
living practice,
the portal
and it's arcing
destination,
the relentless
discipline
of this
incarnation,
beloved,
arrived.

····•··

This is the
essential,
the deep
into
the not knowing,
the
core
so long unrecognized
my feigned
command
lost in
the lostness
my leap
along
the drowning
waters
the shore
so far from here,
the necessary ending,
the wind
without a victor,
the perishment
and the
waves ahead.

· · · · ·●·

This is my body at the never mastering

split

between the coastlines into time places pulling in my intercostals until I lift above the waters and live this way beyond my stamina prophecy of the captivity never captured story and I am The People Could Fly.

· · · · · ·●

I've put
the stretch into
my earth
and now I'm
strong enough to
rise,
history and
certitude
in these limbs
ever upright
as if
I'm suspended
in the knowing
and so I become
a blessed interruption
a single bliss,
an unrest,
the end
of an arrangement,

an arrival.

XXIX

EKA PĀDA RĀJAKAPOTĀSANA

ONE-LEGGED KING PIGEON PREP

216

●······   ·●·····

I have crossed from
a horizontal
life to The Elevation

lift into hidden
panoramas
of blood,
noose,
whip and bone,
Babcock clamp
that tied
the forcing fallopian
knot,
lettuce blade
and razor fork,
cramping thumb
and seizing wrist,
and the fetid stable
welcoming
of Camp Harmony;
I have my view
up spine
hard scale
alluvial vantage
in my space,
in this clearing,
of myth evaporation.

This is my
royal
line,
atypical elegance
of the
vessel non-symmetric,
A fanfare of
differed bones
on a boosted perch
and these limbs
are song,
I have
trained them
by tamp and torque
into a vertical horizon
of such
strange
divinity.

Call my back
the undestroyed
possibility
and my chest
a sacred page.

I cannot be
turned.

My throat is
the lookout.

My gaze
is the pen
and the ink
of my leg
snatches
the well
to the bridge of my nose
and my unbreaking.

I will do
the telling
and

I am unwritten.

My gathering up,
vertebral stack
and sealing skin
are the living wage.

This is the
deserving
rise,
how it feels—
and in all the care
we give,
the shattered hipped
and soon forgetting,
children of
the double shifted,
in all this
I organize myself
for the torso
and
its cup
of a new,
requited age.

· · · · ● · ·

I am fresh
up
from the undreamed
and living,
tested,
earned this holding
gaze,
muscle and plume,
tone of the survivor,
better than the
myth
and its collapse.

I'm upright
and long.

I'm what
comes next.

Sovereign.
Back body singing
and a wallop
in my throat.

My front knows
all sides
and yet
I'm unnegotiated.

My pose is pre-Pinta,
my coast is defended
and I, at last,
am the first
and

the welcoming.

Once sod,
ever earth,
farmer of the 21st
by the fair fees
my ancestors
dare not charge
but I am naming them.

I pose my back
into a farmer's wage,
a pride of spine,
a master view
of each typography,
a knowing
and its many
resolutions.

My knee
taps soil
as my posture
snap rises
into a bold re-appropriation
of what you
once made low
and I call it,
I regal it,
yard work.

XXX

EKA PĀDA ADHO MUKHA ŚVĀNĀSANA

ONE-LEGGED DOWNWARD-FACING DOG

222

●······

One leg listens
and
the other
is traveling
feed the
femur
for the
ilium news.

Bone deaf
daddies
litter the ground
but my heel
denies them
heel denies them
and the false
that they
told.

One leg travels
like a tendon
of angel,
attendant of angel
on a wide
angle lens
and the shin
is the short
of the juice
and
the see
to the life
and the dangle
and swift eulogy.

I got gift
in my split
I got listen
and limb and
ground no one
gave us
ground
no one gave us
and ahead
to the shift
ahead to the shift,
ground
no one save us—
ahead

to the shift.

There are
those of us
who live
in migration,
who stake
and move,
carry the gifts
of ground,
then rising
always
the ground
then rising
and if
you herald
this agility
we will last together,
allies of
a pollinating
wind
adept and
hearty
in an
age

of extinction.

This is my body
that won't be
forgotten,
in the herding,
in the
claustrophobic squares
and digital locks
in the relentless
arbitrary campaigns
to own
this burnished skin,
to bind these ankles
with no chance of flight
and this
is why my knee
is rising
above my head,
an article of sky,
a sound wave,
a letter
to my daughter,
a black beret
on a ten-point landing

at Market and 55th.

Down here
in the low
of my two-gender
knowing,
lulled
in
infinite shade,
a range rises
above my torso,
one heel roots,
but the other
is traveler
strives for more
than
the constant valley
and for once
my body
is listening
to people
of such subtle
and dramatic sweep

and sudden elevations.

Gonna follow
my dancing leg
while my other
joint lays down
the needle
and I'm one
and about
home and away
back spin heel
of the quick mix
theory
to the metatarsal rise
of the
furious five.

Two beats long
while my
palms
keep it steady.

Hell,
I am the
original dog.

We who have waited
and we who have not,
live in the
one body
deep
into
the standing ground
heel pierce
among the rail spikes
hook pulleys
and keening bones
of the once not yet past
and the lifting hope
defiant elevation
of the any means
pelvic to ankle
liberating span
that takes
its own air
toward a liberation
unknown.

This new world earth
don't resolve,
lingers
like a diminished
seventh once
I spread my tips
and go my octaves
down.

I'm taking my pain
from the bones
and singing it,

I'm swinging
my leg
like a tibia suite
and you can bebop this
or cakewalk that
but the blood ground
is always humming
it's dictation and
I am the one that takes
the music round
and if it stings
well —
best be feeling it.

XXXI

UTTHITA HASTĀSANA
IN TĀḌĀSANA

MOUNTAIN WITH
EXTENDED ARMS

228

●······

Know me
by my stand,
sheer drop and
sudden ledges
by the very
face of me
and this look of
"not one more step".
I am the song defense
of rivers,
a punch of bones
aligned,
a searing pitch,
the crystal
and it's cousins,
a thousand
into one,
a stand.

This is but
a preparation,
a toe to finger
foot to sky
topography,
a bone-map
of the unknown country
that brought
these gifts
of practice and
I am hollowing myself
with every reach
with every tumble brush
of word,
of wind
of this history shared
and stolen
passed on and taken
heightening
my body into switchback
learning paths
at old growth angles

and while I cannot block
the haulers,
their spoils
and their caravans,
they will not
go through me.

My length tells you
all you need
to know,

take the long way.

You will know me
with effort,
not be
an easy horizon
not accommodate
the flattened line
of your hopeful sight.

This is seismic
practice
and we
who earn it
live the elevation
and savor
the winding evolutions
put into our bones
by the hidden grace
of strange and powerful
geometries
that grant us more
than our simple limbs.

We are the new ones
who will not shrink
to save you
who keep on
with this rising,
who learned the
molten truth
and use it
who love our way
into the fire
and set the names right
like cooling stone
who cry Patañjali
into the canyons
and put an end
to the lazy passes
and where these mats
are laid and
when
this earth
has changed…

· · · ● · · ·

· · · · ● · ·

I stand
among those
of us
who have always
done
but never been,
the named,
the titled
the rush the din

the unlistening
steep of my back,
the towers I gaze from
the fore of my head,
the air between us,
the snows without a listener,
this life of blind and bound ascendance

and all I yet
would gain
without
my saying.

I am
this sacred,
this olive back,
unmarked,
these wrists
without ligature
this womb
and all my choices
these limbs,
covered or free,
these tighter curls
for my hands alone,
this throat
and all its gifts of truth,
this gender
I have spoken
into light,
these grand making
fingers without censor,
this fist and open palm,
this face of my elders
without apology,
these heels
and this footing,
a dawning reclamation,
this chin
an upward tilt,
to name the missing
and called them home,
this defiant
length
that will not be displaced.
I am a one thousand
year return,
a breathing landform
the majesty,
the living prāṇāyāma –
eruption
and it's
verdant outcome.

Sacred.

······•·

We,
the siblings
and cousins
of the Indus Valley
stand,
mats below,
highlands,
all of us, inheritors
of these steep philosophies,
grand bodies
of the story
centered in the picture,
wherever your camera wanders

centered in the picture.

······•

I am
a living
pan formation,
lived amongst the convex
longitudes and latitudes
scaled an octagon
of pleasures
to know each and every
tender face
and still
you take
one view
of me.

I have learned this –
a mountain knows
no other way
but to be out-
in all directions
at once.

XXXII

VṚKṢĀSANA

TREE

234

●······

What of the
root system
that joins us all
at the palms
of our feet
and the anguished
perishments
and covert survivals
that search through
these tarsals
like hidden code?

Believe. Believe
that we know
each other
at the invocations,
water blessings
canoe journeys and
scoring stones
of the rabbit proof fence.

We live in
a soil without words,
of miracles
after the genocide failed
of more than ourselves—
to mean you with your
weary invincibles –
magnificent and maligned
standing ankle,
of a lifted generation
breathing these
vascular songs
in the one strong limb
while the other rests,
of this reunion
between the buried causeways,
a pride of branches
all speaking in no language
and one tongue.

This is the live
past,
the dead belly night
of a songless sky,
the stasis limbs
before the wind,
the no dawn coming soon
the cambium promise
suspended
the faltering recall
of the swift
and Wren
and in this unrustle,
the canopy
and faith.

This,
below me
is for my children,
precious shade
in a nation
of brutal light,
of sanctioned,
instant triggers,
of agents sworn
to the causes of a strange
and alien sun,
to a fire and pounding
bereft of illumination.

I have found the mother wells,
tapped the distant conifers
built my deciduous blooms
and bring this gift –
for as long
as these limbs
shall live.

··•···

I live
and it's not
for your giving.

I've got reasons
so much bigger
than to be your page,

I breathe cuz
that's what I do.

I'm not your
favorite story
of bringing life
to you.

I talk along the air
and through
the underground
I'm a constant rustle
but not the sound

I'm not the bones
of the house you build

I live like home
in my every day
and I'm good
with that
and not you're
giving.

···•··

Some of us are
mysteries
in standing
eclipsed of daily light,

forested in deprivations
certain to list
and splinter
cleave and tumble flat
below the understory
and yet this
ankle
abdomen and thigh
this mind beyond gravity
this nourishment of line

Speak me in syllables
of vertical and rise

See me of balancing
and miracle
of life,
unfallen.

· · · · · ● ·

My body
is the rising marker,
a narrative and
it's fractal branches
of the perished –
the names—
black men and women
lost to us in this killing age.

Seeing me move
above the gravestone
inert
into a steady
living will
and pollination,

gather into my canopies
and know
that you are spoken
never silenced –
you are spoken.

· · · · · · ●

My body is my
voice.

My hands and face
are an honesty,
rarely holding,
mostly sending
these swift and
changing songs
of the feeder root.

I have put limbs
to this,
language,
as you call it
but too much of me
to name this
in a simple tongue

I am a way
in what you
think is silence;

I am a way.

XXXIII

GARUḌĀSANA

EAGLE

240

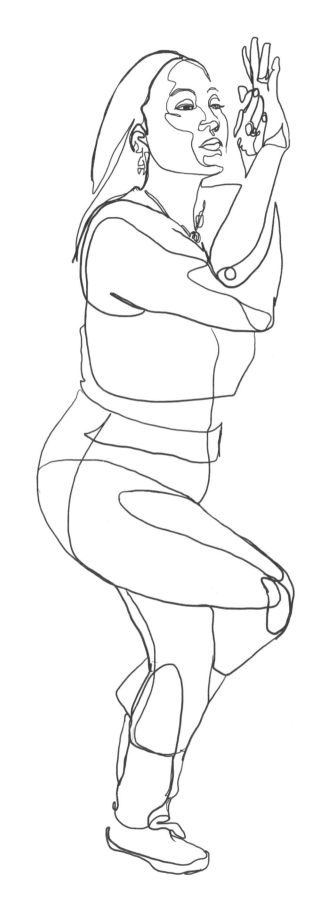

●·····

I am the original
at the perch
before the bigger boats
gathering these wings
for when
the gales
rise.

·●····

These wings
for open air
for thermal
skill and rise

will not be
left upon
a perch of secrets

I am the telling
when I out stretch,
the telling

the taking
of these spaces stolen,

the reclamation
of
my body
and lightened bones –
this balance and
its' coiling are
caught between my lats

but not for long
because what flies
in me
no longer needs
this rest and is
not best
in silence.

Me like the nation,
potential coil
of wing,
aching, knowing I was
meant for
exquisite stretch
when that passed
through lost generations
reaching my scapula range
and we who
are not ready—
give way.

I've got one
thousand goddesses
perching on
my clavicle
like plumage,
and I can't name
them all.

Some of them
are angry
would leap and plunge
into the guts
of the desk and chair
tear the ceilings
from the studs
and some are
healing
while they wait
breathing like
thermals
along the burdens
and the shoulder ache,
some are venting,
some spitting
others writhing
and a few of them
are writing
all of this down.

I can't name them
but one of me
was built for joy
and sings along
the tips of my skin
and none of them
believes
in original sin.

I've got names
I can't recall
but this fierce
insistent lift
of me
is party to them all.

Behold this miracle
of my entanglements
an impossible
avian suspension,
a single talon grips
upon the narrow jut,
the long years
of reading the wind
and the majesty
of my unraveling,
all holding
at once
as time's equals.

The wing and rush
are near and soon
I will have no
lingering talent
for certainty.

You cannot feel the
wing in me
by the shakes and twitches,
tremors, slurs, and jolts
are not the
tellers of my span,
they are the twists
and coils,
the merciless abductions,
the convolutions,
accidents and echoes

but set within me
is the raptor's dream
the grace and bank
the sharp intention
the intercept
the master angle
and outmatched
quarry and the
concentration.

This body
has taught me
to kill
my own surrender
and win.

. . . . . .●

Let me settle
into the not knowing
of this perch and
let my eyes love
my body into stillness.

Once raised oblivious,
I have roosted
at the higher ground

and from this vantage
comes the blood of the better story
like pages just beneath the
loam and dust,
now unburied
I suspect the evidence
at a thousand paces;
I listen to the
well below
and my mind
at every limb is ready –
the spread –
the trajectory –
the gathering and lift,
I have become a creature
of such sight
and finish
and a predator to myth.

XXXIV

NAṬARĀJĀSANA

DANCER

●······

To govern.
To govern

the weep
and missing
of my working
limbs,

to call
this assembly
and coax
a never seen
elegance of democracy
into a sturdy
standing
form

to live my
body
as a leader
and it's cast,

to countenance
and coalesce

into an earning faith
and
flying joy,
to discipline these
aching bands
and set the
stricken free
to take
my sentience and
ascendance
seriously
to make this
my constitution

to govern.

I got three limbs full of rise and reach and
a heel down deep a heel down deep

Put my face into "miles"
and "to go"
and before
and before
and before

then I sleep

my dark is
my me
and
my me is
my deep.

Are you up
for
the new leg?

Are you up
for
the new leg?

Are you lovely and steep?

Are the monuments down?

Is there dust on your feet?

The keep of my promise—
The rise and the reach

and at last and at honest
a heel down deep
a heel down deep.

I live in this body
of the
not two answers
of the glorious discovery
still rising
of the grace
and androgynous bloom,
of nothing
you can nameplate
of the considerable range
of my soon
and later,
and ain't I
just about the
most beautiful body
and beyond it
and never been
my body
and always been
before me
and the one leg
source and solid down,
the rest of me flying
Lord Shiva
force and formless
soul on wheels
gender daring
dancer
that you have ever seen?

Let me show you
how the beautiful end
the struggle into bloom
the outcome of this body
at purpose
the divinity of tendons
the grace
of certain bones
let me show you
that migrations
are nothing to fear
that the stories
begin at the ankle high
and find an arching
strength,
that with the proper tending
I wend and flex
and last relax
into this lush
of miracle,
of evidence
of overstory
and
verdancy.

This is my body
in its original voice,
before I doubted my limbs
and silenced my lyric spine.

This is the recovery,
the answered
quest
the
courage faith
of vertebral intent
bold leg
to the wind,
a remembering,
this is the outstretch
once the doubting fails
and the strong of me
takes its place
on the singing ground.

I stand in my
root
and the bound
of my reach;

I will not be nullified.

I was here
before you named
and unnamed me

and I have built
my immunities.

This body revived
its truth
despite the
wars against me
and now I shrink
for no one,
I swell into a discipline
of reclamation of dance
of once and never –
a constancy.

I cannot be

nullified.

Let us dance
on this
without hyphenation,
absent of compounding
interests
and call it
what it is.

Race.

See my limbs
conquer your equivocations
and rise into the raw
of it
and when you see
a warrior divinity –
concede this
globe
to the

higher ground.

XXXV

VĪRABHADRĀSANA III

WARRIOR III

252

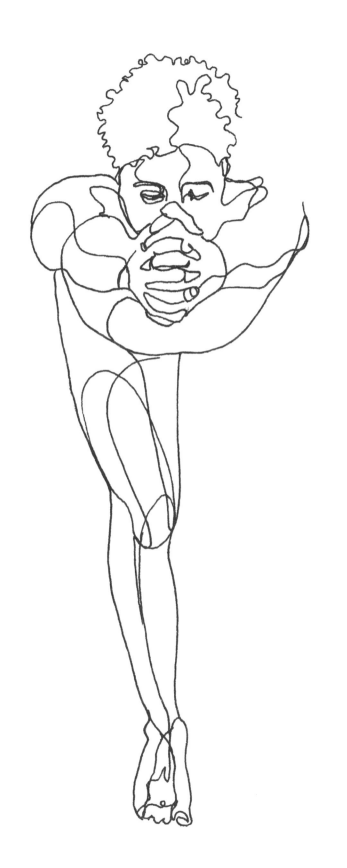

●······

At even.
Neither upright nor supplicant.
Level
The trained back to hold this horizon.
The need to face it squarely and the bones to make it work.
A levering to rightness.
A call to the long sought balancing plane up.
Long.
Lasting.
At even.

I'm following
the water,
the tongue
and sweet of it
at the front
of my chin,
the chime
of the hidden well
in the hollow,
my shin
the tremble fret
wet and ringing,
and the sweet of my belly
torso stretched
like a tremor string.

Who sings these waters
and who is forbidden?
Whose spigots are cursed
by the midnight truck
and its toxin dump
and all the dam
and draught diversions?

If I make
my body into this following
what will I taste,
what will I drink,
what is the lime and bitter
the poison
the clear and chosen,
the treble clef,
the condensation?

I rise from the desks,
the confining chair,
the ruler to slap away
my original tongue,
the assimilation
the metallic shorn
and weeping braids,
the Religion
that had no place
in my chest,
I rise from this
and listen to the earth,
to the longest call
to the better education
to the all along me
sifting into prairie sage
in the tall grass thick,
un-hostaged.

Warrior.

• • • ● • • •

• • • • ● • •

Put me at the shore.
Facing.

This is the stand of the
change comes
and the last leg
of the old beliefs
in their suspension

of
a strange,
intended rise
of a parallel,
but not familiar

of how
brave holds

a breath or
so
into
astonishment.

· · · · ·●·

On this day
my spine is clear
and my anchor
leg does
not negotiate.

I am taking
the horizon
in memory
of those denied it,
setting my exquisite lengths
into this once

and better leveling.

· · · · · ·●

I test my sternum
and
rest of my throat
plumb
along the common ground
in prayer with
a billion bodies
all bowing like
suspended arrows,
coiling in a
perfected bow

"In due time"
is dead—
instead
aloft
swift no waiting

now.

XXXVI

VĪRABHADRĀSANA I
WITH GARUḌA

CRESCENT /
HIGH LUNGE
WITH EAGLE ARMS

258

This is the
strong in me.
Placed.
Not advancing
but advanced.

I'm not going anywhere
but here,
with you-
in this,
from the bottom
of my knee
to the mist
of my cranium sutures.

Stepped.

Out.

Past the inward edge
of the indigenous frontier.

Ground to be
named
but until then –
Justice.

No more.
None of the
daily violences
None of the
taking ground
I call my body
The no end
to these violations
and demeanments
must be ended.
And the strength
of us
all
who know the difference,
we are one together
in defense,
set to a common leg
against all trespass
one stride
of a tandem army.

Decisive.
Set.
No more.

･･●････

Calves locked
at long last
dawn.

Advance and
survivance –
that's my people
at their first
and second leg.

This body
is my story,
a telling,
a claim –

I will not perish.

･･･●･･･

Today I am
the finding,
the body of
the indigenous,
the strength
of the refusal,
the witness,
the abrogation of complicity,
the mattering,
the definitive end
of the age of the missing—
the visible high ground

I state
into embodiment.

Now to interrogate
the over ground,
a step beyond
denying of the Jim Crow
and apartheid
of this hidden
savage
modern day.

I build a new keening
base of seeing
and mark the
mournful distances
of race.

I know these
deprivations depend
upon my constancy

of retreat

a conditioning
my body longs
to break
beyond all comforts
and by this steady lunge
I sing

"I am here
at the anguish
of a distance
I must change."

I step into
a higher silence
and the let the cacophony resolve
without me.

I am not your
market body,
your ears and eyes
to win a thousand times
each day.

I am the force
of my own company
a settlement of solitude
on this jealous plane
and I find my own antiquities
coursing through the
femur range
rising to the
ancient brain
of my middle chest
resting
unsettled
without the pitch
of arsenal distractions.

I am here
in the older words
in the thermal winds
in the brutal quiet

and
the lifting.

．．．．．．●

I step strong
into the hidden isolations
just below the
rising eye and I
un-safe
my comfort pose,
extend into lonely places
and know that
so many souls
live achingly apart,
without,
and why not me
to breach in answer
to enter and reduce
by one
the desperate solitude?

XXXVII

EKA PĀDA ADHO MUKHA ŚVĀNĀSANA II

ONE-LEGGED DOWNWARD FACING DOG (HIP OPENING VARIATION)

265

●······   ·●·····

I am the engendering,
the call to unbury,
the revelation of uproot,
the earth here
at my fingertips
with all its stories
never said
but through me
un-hostaged.

I am the truth
of my underbody
at peace with my orientation,
un-bullied,
gathering at the turn,
collecting into unison,
all of my people in me

exquisite answer
to the violence
that once forced
our false apology.

None given now.

I am the
engendering.

What will come
of this opening
I make,
of this quivering
to hold myself wide?

This is a time
for the narrows
in me, for the
unsettling grace of a
quarter twist,
the rise and rush
and an unexpected
steepening.

Courage sends
it up beyond
the certainties,
past the grounding comforts
into the never named,
the cosmology
that seeks the very plexus
of our hips and groin.

We are first and most
a child to the unknown
and the scale of it
the scale of it
sings beyond
theology.

I take counsel
with the near voices
waning,
and the dead
as a practice of inversion
a listening
to the precious branch
of days just
beneath the common plain
and every grief
and joy
in this demand
an opening
make room
for my return
in the quarter spiral
of hips and relief
of one less secret
and one more sky

to tell.

・・・・●・・   ・・・・・●・

Essential contact
and a keen,
this is my daily,
the pleading
that stalk the words in me,
the stories spread
along the ground
and seize the metacarpal
and co-opt them
into a scripted discipline
of writer,
teller,
journalist,
griot
and all the other names
of and toward
this jubilant
misery,

So many silences to fix,
so many risks in the fixing,
and the next turn,
always the next turn.

The lineage is
best learned low –
under the high poses –
by the flat of the toes
and round
of the fingers
where I listen
with my skin and limbs
and trust the
humbler numbers
of those who gather with me
at the pace of this earth

and my teachers
are rarely the
darlings of the market –
they bring demands
from the
bones of the soil
and lose their share
of supplicants
in the name of rigor

and we have years
to share between us
my teachers and I

and poses to hold
and exquisite tomes
to carry
in our wrists
and write into

our hips.

･ ･ ･ ･ ･ ･●

She has never left
this ground
and I am
not so different.

She has never
left this ground
and so I am
organizing;

She has never
left this ground,
me,
an audience
with this inaudible divinity
in my bones,
the cool
and dew
and grains
and grooves –
so much between us
and those who leave her
will live by calamity

but my shins and wrists
know better take me
to this next beginning.

She has never left me.

XXXVIII

AṢṬĀṄGĀSANA

EIGHT POINT

270

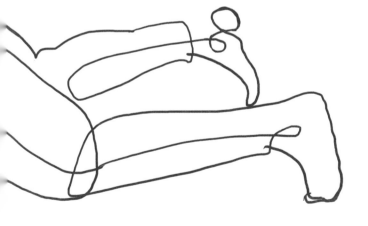

I was raised
with one story,
sunk myself into
a truth solitude,
grew from a
single blessed view.

And there it is –
like many,
to the end of my days.

But this business
of the seven silences
seeping into elbows
shaking my resting knees
gathering these palms
in the dust
toes scraping
an asphalt dawn
just below the bullet casings

and I am freed of my comfort

unfused

many parts digging
a tendon listening
that means trouble
and leads a fire chorus, wild,
into my bones.

I rest in this today's body
with all its width
and length,
quivering
shoulder strength,
belly kissed
along
the loving ground
and I keep the
sound of
my breathing,
a chime
of sternum prayer,
and it's all there –
the fat and weathered creases,
the friction,
it's irritation
and releases
of pulse
and pulse
and heat
my resolution –
a metronome of skin
and lay me
down the rivers
let me sing
the wild
the pleasure
of this body
and soaring imperfections
never will
I leave you
and lay me down
the river
with all its
width and
length.

This is my
daily grounding,
a cultivation of rigor –
the trinity of science, fact
and history
and these pursuits
demand
no halfway,
no ease or
distance so I'm down –
steepening,
listening bones
in this perpetual
investigation,
prone to lengths
and the
sweet risks
of each
awakening.

I love in
the views of
the low horizon,
not the meta-heights
and all its
glories,
but the limb and clutter,
the shiver body
tarp spread
and door jam
under the icing
awning
the gritted tents
beneath the
highway pass,
the strike of heel,
scrape of
paddle,
and shifting bow
where this
canoe nation
awaits it's welcome,
the calloused fingers
of the spinach
pickers
who strain their psoas
into ache,
and the asphalt rake
and orange vest of
the public works,
with a pothole
filled
and a thousand
more to go.

This is my
driven place,
and I take
counsel,
birchen gaze,

I hold the line.

I am taking this
turn
I
was never given,
the anthem promises
and pledges
withheld
while I waited
at the
tongue
of the talking earth
along the throat
of
the water
and stretched
my silence
down into my knees
until my chin
was done
brow broken
and such a worthy jaw
to open.

All of you,
so used to talking
dispose yourselves
this is at
long last
the generation
of
interruption.

The turn you've stolen?

I'm taking.

If you look
from here
long enough
you can see
the measure
we've been taking,
the song making at
the soul of
the throat,
the Mississippi Delta
back body
string thrum
at the long
sigh
day,
a tension
at the triple tap
shin
the long stretch
of my gospel hymn
the middle thrash
of the fiddle
notes
permanently
unwritten
all of
them at
dirt level
roots
and binding
just like a
history book
if you look
if you listen
if you look…

• • • • • •●

Break ground
with me.
Dare to surface
and
defend
these once
buried
shoots and
tender sheaths
of a long
and
better way
which sings
it's justice
at just the
proper hour
and the very idea of us
has braced
an elder
overstory
to hoard
the ample light
until these answers
we become
are deprived.

So this breaking
needs all
of us,
not an epic
hero tale,
but a planting
of such scale
that we, for
once,
are
all the
eye
will know.

XXXIX

ARDHA
ŚALABHĀSANA

HALF LOCUST

276

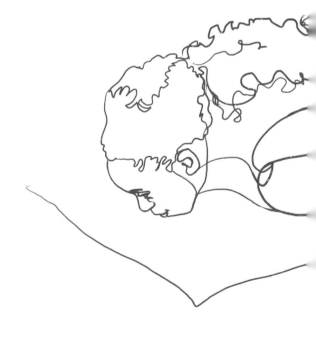

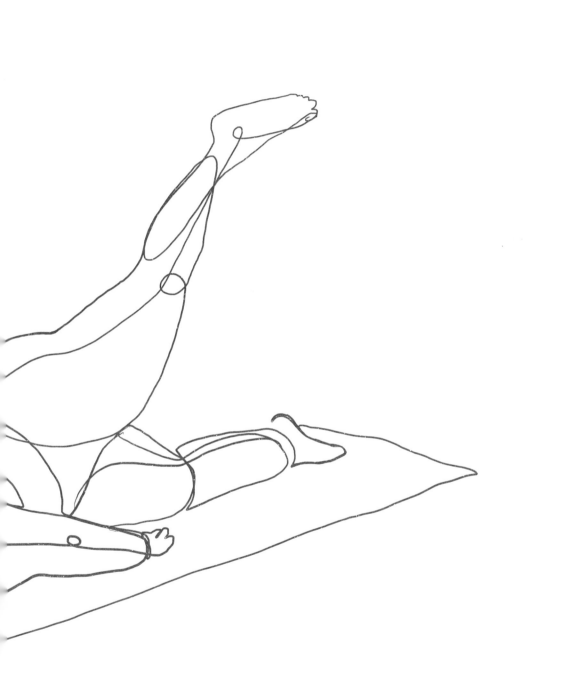

●······

I rise with
what I
have
on these,
the low days
I rise
with what
I have.

These dangers
of
my unknowing
are not
the better mysteries,
make a labyrinth
of my gaze
and it's horizon,
set the
narrow tall
and other me
to constant
strangers.
Against these perils
I rise into
my wilderness
deep into the dorsal
blind
by the courage
of my skin
and just beyond
my stretch −
a finding.

One thing.
Not the many
or the two.
Me as the
instrument
of a single string
my breath as
bow
my song of
faith and bone
along the molecules
and waves
on this first of
morning −
one thing.

Bother with
the first –
the Peoples,
this discipline,
the stranger sounds before
my tongue,
the songs that
ask
permission,
the
single limb
of recognition,
the other seven
in rotation,
the names
in absence
from my books,
the strain
of
how to learn
them all,
the weight,
and how
I lift it,
the elevating grace
and its transmission,
the length
and where
it's hidden
the troubling
and strength
the where behind me
and the length.

This body of
the prone citizen
must end.
This laying low,
this hibernation,
still into silence
civic conditioning
wins an atrophy
of many ages
and on this day
I raise my heavy sleep
set firm
this tremor knee
speak through the
shin of my muster

and make my muscle win.

. . . . . •.

Long ago
I escaped
in plain
sight
fielded the hail
wind whipped debris
and cyclone batter
of dire sentences
on my aftermath
body
and lay
like no space
was too low
like down
was faith
and from the
fleeting
ground
I found
the eye of it –
and never long
relief
but still –
and this has
been
my sleep
a gentle dying,
undetected
a daily weep
supine.

Then.
This misbehaving
limb
this pure addiction
to lift this treason
to the rest
of my docility–
finds the risk
of currents
puts my spine
in opposition
to soft consent,
keeps living off
the comfort ground
until I am
at last
thoroughly unrested
despite my vow
of sleep.

· · · · · ·●

Flatten me.
Press me into dust.

Push my lats
like stone
into the bones
and grains
of the tongue
and groove –
send my nose into it
and I will
learn my buoyancy
raise my shaking calve
rattle my tibia
channel these
propulsions
and make a mockery
of your supremacy.

Covet my
chortle shin.

Go ahead and
dare me down
my glute
is in it now
and in just
a minute
my ass will be
up.

XL

ŚALABHĀSANA

LOCUST

284

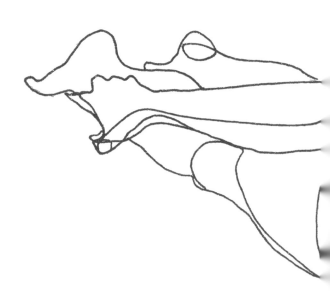

●・・・・・

The last of it –
the who I love,
the how I love
braced into this
greed of wind,
this exhilaration
is cast,
and cleared
and I am a
liberation.

・●・・・・・

My body is
the doctrine
ripe for the
reading,
a perfection
outstretched
that no shame
may enter.

These are my
divine
fibers
the tomes
and
reaches
of
my pelvic
canon
and I am such
strong and sturdy
wonders
to pose.

Once this body
music
and all its
crown
and elevation
synch and
pate and
swank
and
funk –
it's the song
that made me
do it
it's the song
that
wade me
through it
and I got
this
ever life
of blood
and finger bones
of floating
shoulder stones
of ankle evolution
it's the song
that brought me to it
and a long
ascending
and a long
ascending
and a long
ascending.

· · · ● · · ·

Fire for the
bream
and set
my belly
to the wave
bent at holy
camber
I take these
waters back.

You have sprayed
my pools
with acid,
chained me
to the
deck
taunted my
descendants
and leaded
many taps.
But my body
wants
the answers
to swim and
skim
the tide
to fore
against these
shadows
and take
the waters
back.

· · · · • · ·

On my belly
listening to
the mind
I won't ignore,
for the
nourishment a
sugar tongue misses,
for the goodness
in
the curry soup
and pot,
for the sobs
that need
a
throat path
out
for the guts of my
glory
that seek
nothing of
war,
for my solar plexus
trove of dreams
and all its warrior
attentions
for the gorgeous
myth of my
story and the mystic
truth in
my mundanity.

This is my core
flat or rounded
and I shan't forsake
it
on this wide
and
common floor.

· · · · · ● ·

These are the practices
of distribution
which take
such
rigor
and extract such
core.

Breeze of the
ancestors
stalking my heels
seizing
my sacrum
and pumping
my ganglion
with fluid,
urgent matters
along the long
windings of
my vertebral column
and slow
into my
vision horizon
and there is
such
ruptured
earth
before me
and so many
centuries of
leveling
to
go
as the
waters rise
and the
southlands drought
and the last of
the fertile plains
are
taken
so few corners
left for
the rest of
us
stacked

by the
wrongness of blankets
at such odd
angles
and overhangs
huddled masses
everywhere
and me with
a single
metaphor spine
deep into
the evening.
I believe
and extend myself
deep
into
the evening.

· · · · · ·●

This is my pose
of naming myself
of risen strength
against
all binary
coercions,
a torsal
declaration
and I have
outlasted you,
the relentless
who sing your
violence
with oblivious
spite.

I've bested this
false
gravity
this
casual delusion
to right myself
and
become my
own name.

XLI

ARDHA BHEKĀSANA

HALF-FROG

292

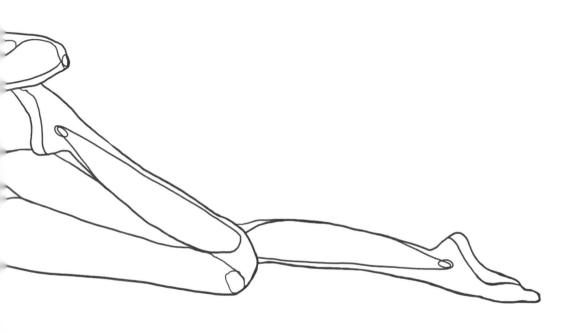

And if I am calling
in that
which I've
left to
secrets in
the public
space,
this essential
sinew
and all these
elegant bones,
I know my
name
and all
the tuck of
cradle strength
carries my
fragile self
until I am outright
at full reunion.

Best to discipline
this unthinking
splay
of my casual limb,
this claim and claim
and claim
again
of every inch
and every domain,
of a mindless
life of trespass,
and for
this once
and forward
fold taut
and check
retract
and
solace
my knee
in
winter,
no hallowed greed
or mystic destiny
my knee
in winter.

··●····

I have seen the
body as
its practiced
the forgotten limb
the rigid lay
of
things without
account
the absence
of muster
and it's
attending
mercies
the indulgence,
the yawn
and the withering
the blithe
descent
into
weighted callosity,
I have seen
this
governing body
with all its slack
and
broken troths
and I am calling in
the dormant sole
the governed
as so
neglected
the last of me
to finally
been made first.

· · ·●· · ·

We the
women
asymmetric
not your
mythic balance
your harmony
all sides
not your gentle bend
or maternal flex
not the saviors of
calming supplication
and all attending
banal civilities
make our bodies
known,
take our side
seriously
call the tarsal
truth
into our spine
until it trembles
up
into our
larynx
and stake a
beautiful,
inelegant
sharp and
fine position,
to shift,
to swift
unballast
action.

We the
women
asymmetric.

· · · ·●· ·

I've forgotten
the bend
and the six
generations
before me,
the gentle,
pulled apart
from we, the male born,
the chronic flex,
fatigue
and hardening
the double book
of victors
wedged
behind the cradle
of
my knees.

I've forgotten that
I deserve
my share
of soft tissue
that I belong
to the
branch
the
willow
and the brook
not just
the stone
that when I
meander
I find my
way back
that the straightest
edge
was never my
map
and when I
return
it will be
at the bend.

· · · · ·●·   · · · · · ·●

What of the   This
skin and   the body
the silence,   this the
my quiver shin   left behind
as   of
an offering   the body
at the   this the distance
palm   of
of the morning   the left behind
and the crow song   this the
in place   governing for
of the phone cack   distance
and the ring tone?   the brazen glee
                           and greed distance
What of the   the distal
solitude   phalanx
in these fingers   the linear
the carry   extremities
of my bones   the dis-invited
the strums of   un-nation
a distant   of a head above
intersection   and then the parts-
and the sudden   I unjoin
truth   and
of a mending   seek a better
quad?   union
                           and reach from
Are not these   and stretch from, and all from all –
the
better pause   for the left behind.
and a
vivid way?

XLII

UTTHITA
ŚALABHĀSANA

EXTENDED LOCUST

299

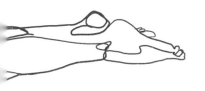

●······   ·●·····

Gut sworn on the
fertile, moist
and
baking ground
there is no end
of
me
no divot
where the rail
of my ancestors
ceases
and mine begins
no acre of
cotton field
that hasn't torn
my fingers
good
no mud barrack
gate
that can't be swung
back open
no muttering of
   "nothing can be
    done"
that can't be
re-sung
no end to the
messenger
below my
belt
kicking a reminder
that every liberty
deserves a
listener
that what passes
is
forever below
us
and even as
my limbs reach
my belly
takes the call.

These arms and
legs
are of my
imaginings
and if
I had but
one
of
two
I would
hold you,
tender my
forearms
to the
small of
your back
into you
felt
the weather of
my orbit
warm your
laughing bones
as if we
were the constancy
of
twin stars
in the play of
reciprocal ellipse
but the blast
of this
is
I am sun
and you are
planets
I count your perigees
like a cherishment of days
and dart about
and I am raging
sharp-
but often rounded
too often rounded
but in
my imaginings…

Warrior of the
colonial winds
I send my
four limbs
to know
what I will
not follow –
the laws
the wars
the profits
and the absence.

I am not their
stranger
they are not my
friend
at
the end of
the
disputed
territories
while my breastbone
does not
wander
from the
original ground
and a
whisper into
the daily hours of my ribs

Here is my center

Here is my center

I am one transmission
despite
the risks,
a ground reporter
limbs at the
forever
tips of
an investigation
unblocked throat
and words,
a flight of
them
in the
names of
the hidden
and the
hiding
and
I have no
mastery of
outcomes
but let the stories fly
let the stories fly
and when the perpetual
violence of
fraternities
raise their weapons
wing my back
wing my back
until the
next
column comes.

· · · · ● · ·

If my pose become
prayer
and my prayer
become being
then I
am
two –
the vaunt of
reach,
the imagination,
the altitude
and arc,
heels and palms,
an effort into
the high
air
and this is
the
first of me – while the
simultaneous second
is spoken belly
deep
in 40 acres of
captivity
in broken soil
a growing
of immense
disputed song
a manipulated longing
and a skin below
me
that seeks its end
in miles
and millenniums
and yells
through the
crack in my chest
"keep going".

Long-ago the
Word
became my
earth
and my bed,
repetition
my every morning—
one among divinity –
home.

But these arms and
legs
are wiser than
my chest
disdain
my hard earned
certainties
squeeze past
my theologies
and given boundaries
and enter
into
a pervasion of
turbulence
of rattling compassion
and curiosity
of fingertips
that love
the
mess
just within
my
reach
and insteps
straining
for a single
taste
of
the
other ground.

Let me pull my
heart into
the necessities
of my intersections,
center gravity
and
my outer-reaches
limb – finger—
shin—toes
of such
divine
multiplicity
and I will not
surrender
the living system
of
my skin
or the muscle
of
my memory
I am the
proud paradox
simultaneous
living it out
all at
once.

XLIII

DHANURĀSANA

BOW

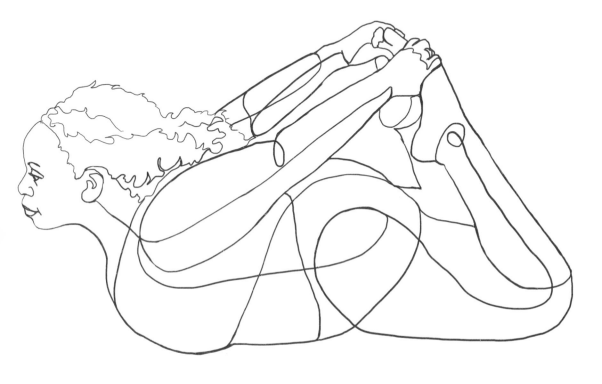

●······   ·●·····

Life at the back of
me
is older than friends
believes in
circles,
sings in
wending
blues
to mend
the ruptures
frees my
ankle
wrists
to build
reunions
and claims
this
better living
systems
supreme.

I am not
the acquiescence
I am not the
supplication
I am not
his body bound
I am longer
I am rounder
I am free.

I am perfecting
the anger of
my bearers,
cycling it into the
bones of my
shoes and
the court of my
palms,
squeezing sense
out of my innocent
shins and
wringing
a verdict
that brings no
comforts of
the smaller
solution.

I am the bigness
of
the unrest,
it's occasional
bending beauty
the question
raw
the violence
made into light.

This struggle
this double bind
this unknowing
these flare of
limbs
do not often
live
in the
necessity
of my uncertainty
of the discipline
the humility
sustained
and how have
I let
my sprawl
come to this?

How long have I
ignored
the indwelling
discomforts
of my better
reach?

What will come
of
me if I
seal
my
infinite
escapes
take
my grip
of justice
and hold
myself to it?

And as for my hair
it is final
texture
always good
and glory
and only I - these, mine
the privileged
hands — there are
no exceptions
sovereign
all of me —
it is final.

. . . . • . .

Supremacy of head
ignorance of shin
of flex
of abdomen
and ankle—
these are no
accidents
but the thoughtless
rigors
of my kind
and many
a common
distancing
to keep my
skin
apart
from the grip
and
know
of a
story
I am not
listening
seeps
I am not
listening
sleeps to
wake
in ways
I wish were
hidden
while the story
sows
itself into
my palms.

Unity is not
a
silent thing –
it is loud,
it is grip
and loss
and ankle deep to knee –
and not
getting
out of this
so easily
once I risk
this mess
of
reach.

· · · · · ● ·

Stave and string
I am
for the
nock
the fit and
feather shaft
the sinew
set for
launch
the belly
and the
grip
the fiercest
to
the sun
the plunge
the death
of falser
heroes
that have lived
too wrong
upon this earth
I live between
the curve
and sharp
and you will
know me
from
this story
until another
nock
is ready.

·····•

I.
So long have I
been facing West
in seeking myth
of this horizon,
belly down
strafe and rake
across the plain
perfect my
harrow
claim
of inadvertency see
until what fallows
until what fallows
my gaze was high
but never true.

II.
My legs,
my root
are dis-remembered
behind, unseen
gravity tossed
along this half-life
splayed
sinking
mine and ours —
the settlers —
and ever after
and over soon
and never or
and soon to settle.

III.
What I leave behind
what I will not see
unsettles me,
until I'm left
with further
West
or reaching blind
for all of my
forgotten body
a risk
of awkward limbs
a first and
early bending,
a grasping
ache,
a beauty
meant to
tears,

a symmetry.

XLIV

CATURAṄGA DAṆḌĀSANA

FOUR-LIMBED STAFF

312

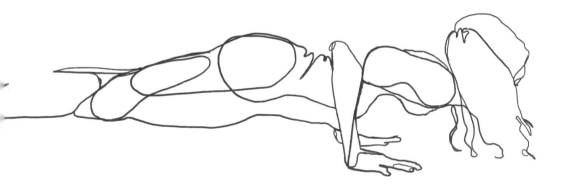

● · · · · · ·   · ● · · · · ·

I hover low
condition strong
on the whisper plane
in the unguarded
territories
and we have
this song of camouflage
mine of melanin
and you
of heart
that blister rambles
along your tongue
like some glad
confession
from the blooded
barely hidden tomes
of othering.

And I see you
and mark the message
at
this double
passing.

I am no
accident
of stillness,
these privacies
these boundaries
of my culture
are the absolute rights
of my inner space

and you have
no purpose there

without

my consent.

··•····

This lowering is
not submission –
I am in
the listening
the territories
of transmission,
the muscle suspense
of a holding there
toward a way
that will not rise
in me
before the endurance
and the play
of this descent

and I am long in this
like the ones
that came before me

I am long
in this.

··· • ···   ···· • ··

We are never above
the water –
best to live
even with it
friend ourselves
to these surging,
waning
coiling songs
as if the
octave arteriole
were singing them.

Make this elonging,

this torso
a living filter
and answer
to artery Earth
to her clouded worry
and alien particulates
until the vast hectare
of these finger creeks
spread across our capillaries
throttles every liter
of our liquid belly
and take
us down –

even.

I am the interruption;

violence is passed
by generation
across the muscle line
end here
before the
next collapse.

My children
deserve my
strength
and I have it
this holding,
this miracle
of mid-air
that I've become
and all the gifts
of stamina
a spending wrist of
daily kindness
and faith of palm –

a decision.

· · · · · ●·   · · · · · ·●

I am going to
try living
at the low words,
the few
the awkward still
the many pauses
like fingers spread
across the earth
the gifts at
the black
of things
the antonyms of sky,
the multitude of grubs
and all these
messy democracies.

What is this
permanence of visitor
that has never been
my wisdom
and why has it taken
so long
to un-home myself
and silent
and strange
and just the first
of any
un-centering?

How many billion of
us
are left to the low
with full throats,
songs along
the muscle bones
of our hidden wings
and a government
of listeners
who love the
silence?

We make no peace
along this

pressed horizon.

XLV

SĀLAMBA
BHUJAṄGĀSANA

SPHINX

318

●·····

We who look
the white
and prone
to live the part
attended to
the ground
and sound
to sleep
head to stone
and nothing rising
sink our temples
into fallow crusts
of plain
into this cloaking
shackle bargain
into a silent
life
unspoken
and there she rests
and there he tarries
and how
they test
the racist registries

of
all these chaste
delimiters
lids to earth
and
lips to dust
and
so much of us
empty of horizon,
until this
spine
this belly
of
seeded story
this language
in my throat
this wild frontal
skull
that wants
the light and
bends me up
into a distant
answer
and
fiercer question.

After prayer and
the full supplication
comes the rising;
my open throat
and all the risks
of my raw divinity,
these emissary wrists,
and my spine
just warming.

The body is my word
The body is my word
and on this day-

I shall not rest.

My bones know
the deck
whether wood
or iron.

I am prone
to no soft landing,
and to coastal crests,
and restive winds
and harbors
that were anything
but safe to me.

Once forced below
I took my hour of light
and made it
into
centuries.

I stared down
the leaping waters
and did not
leave my
breath
I won this lift
and vision
from the tower
of my ribs
and whispered
to my children
to weld another
deck
to seek
a different bay
to fire up the
steel
to liberate this vessel.

··· ● ···   ···· ● ··

Me and we-   Upon this elbow-wrested
the face-   ground
no apology   I am lineage,
sienna umber   successor,
olive sable   the wisdom,
obsidian   a breathing trust
or fleet mahogany   the given way
latte chest   a new grace
and an   and I will not squander
isthmus   this lifted
in my soul   recognition,
I take a
couple continents   but rise
to cross;   through my crown
                            and follow
I know   the line.
you ain't feeling
me
if you live
a land-locked gaze
I'm river
I'm coastal
I'm days—
an answer
you won't be
looking for,
in front of
you
the septum pierce,
the zaftig lips
the face-

no apology.

. . . . . ●.

From here
I can see
all of you
your beginning
body,
the open galaxy
beneath
your eyes,
the sweet pea bud
of your early
breath
and the casual twist
and give
in your hair.

This is my
renewal,
you in full
before me,
the arrival of
my once forgotten

prayer.

. . . . . .●

I'm listening to
the old medicine,
the pulse and report,
the plants, the herbs
and all their clemencies
the glare down
of a raven
on a winter logging road,
the paddle slice
of my song canoe,
the intercostal clearings
and their blessed ventilations

the common patch
and all its miracles,
the story
that was never meant
but here I am

the dwindling abundance-

the medicine.

XLVI

SUKHĀSANA

GOOD-SPACE

325

●······

I am the
act of
creation and knowing-
the seat,
I have chosen
the beginning –
the writ,
the lap
the bud
the stem
the "I am"
there is no
naming me
until my name
and I think
I am Genesis
the chapter
it's author,
the mudded waters
the kichad
vitality,
a groin
a slough-
divinity
and I am
still
in naming
the risen
and the
up rising.

·•·····

You may have
noticed
over several hundred
years
that I cannot
be unearthed,
that my ass
incarnates
in the
next generation
and reclaims
original ground
that I love
this
seat and
you can't have it,
that each eradication
brings the next
return
that my resting knees
are wiser than your
active plow
that these
ankles mighty
have loosened
at just the
best angle
that I am
divine geometry –
an answer
infinitely solved.

..●....

We are the ilium
of the
national bones,
the race? –

Belong-,

so call me
by my name.

We have stacked
kilometers
into our femur bells
and they are still
ringing
stored the seven
days
of highest sun,
repeated,
into this
melanin of resilience
and become
the seated
a virulent
resistance
to much
bestial, wishful
unimagining
until that word
is bullied
from existence.

We are high space
sung down
to iliac crest
a maximus staying
and the ground feels
fine to us
so in your failed
binary
we are never two
and only one –
Belong.

Call us by
our
name.

··· •···   ····•··

Pistil, stamen,, ovule,
stem,
I am origin –
a unity,
the first body
and I am surrounded
by my prevalence-
the waters
and the loam
I am soil –
an estuary,
the yawning spring
and don't I sit pretty?

An open lap
in an age
of storms.

Vow about to
sit into this –
not the calisthenic –
not the strive
or conquer
but the settled
intimacy
over time –
the revelations
my body
counts
when
the clock stops,
and the line insinuates
along my
bones
until my lap
finally softens
and I am
a cistern
to the falls
and

way.

·····•·   ·····•

This is the pose
of the
my body
as I settle
into the
having wept
and the saline sea
and my lap
and the impossibility of my
strong and casual spine.

These are my limbs
in the tension
of rest
after the tuck
of survival
and now to
the mended angles
and my wrists
and rediscovered
ankles
me of the
my body
my body

violenced-

and against this sin
not did I end
a stranger to myself
and I raged
and I wept
and I rose
and the salinity.

This is the pose.

Will you accommodate
the original set,
or do I sit
despite your design
against me? –
a long complicity
of innocence
that forms an
absolution
so concise
that you make
no room for the
very dissent
of
my existence
my entrance
on wheels,
my limb finger face
trilogy voice of
choreography
and my louder
etiquettes
that don't
match the
pervasive silences
of an implicit law
that does
not meet my consent.

Do I wait?
and I will not
so here I
sit
permanent.

I leave you
to your explanations.

XLVII

ARDHA MATSYENDRĀSANA

HALF LORD OF THE FISHES

332

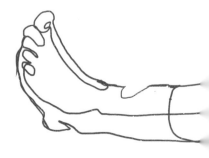

This is the turn,
my life outside
the corridor.

These are my
strategies ended
and how my
torso
runs curious
to this strain
and my glance
at strangers
and no evidence
of
the other.

Once into this
earth body
which I
somehow denied
at constancy,
made a life of
fore and aft,
gazing,
while the peripherals
accumulated
like a vast
micro plastic surf,
on an ocean column,
or the land bound
ash
of an arctic fire,
twice into this
nerve and thicket,
a little less
shore,
waters rising
and the din
gasp and gale
of a breath
I'm no longer holding.

··●····

I've taught my
spine
to dig into
a hundred rotations
to live away
from home
to name the secret
distances,
to learn the
necessities of
tension,
and to call my
torso into
your sense of center.

I've spiraled
into a
stable multiplicity
coaxed past my
limits
toward infinite
literacies
and I am
the turn,
the rigor-
an answer,
tensile shoulder,
muscle,
the leader
you've
been yearning
for—

I am the turn.

···●···

(For Toni Morrison who lived and lives.)

Let us talk to each
other
in a tongue
that savors us
with fifteen stories
living in our gums,
two shins ready for
the dawn
just before light
and a language
that beats the
sky
to the shore.

We are the people
of recipes
that cannot
be stolen,
we keep them
in our hair,
the dark between
our ribs and my soft
patella
mirrors yours
the way
sisters do
so I will
set the oven
and cook the
pages
sweet and generous
like my carrot
cake and
let the icing
slide down
our throats
and never
answer any questions

except our own.

· · · · ● · ·

You say it sweet,
like a virtue—
"team player";
my body becomes
your ground
to rigid gaze
and the hopes
of new dominion.

I have eyes
on the
left and right horizons
away from
you,
toward a morning
star
that rises in my
throat
until my body
sings "no";
keep your fucking phrase and fable.

I have eyes
on
the morning star.

• • • • •●•

Try a day on
the peripherals,
where you will find
us
not for some
salvation
or to flash
in spiral
out of debt,
not in common sympathy
but simply
in the cause
of stop looking
straight ahead,
ignore the lure
of the line you're
taking
and feel the corners
of the world,
the tight white sheet
of the hospital fold,
the check mark smudge
on the men's room   the skip and the tango
on the duty roster,   of the pink sock
the pleated cuff   kitty ear
off the wrist   brown girl in
of the wine server,   the bagel shop
the missed stem   with her blonde mom trailing
on your pack blueberries, try it and
the exhaustion,   leave it
all around us,   at the top
exhaustion,   of your spine,
                           the choke of
                           your throat and the
                           beaded dew
                           along your waist.

                           Roll the sweat
                           along your fingertips
                           and taste.

                           The edges are the corners,
                           not the prayers.

                           Stop living the
                           straight ahead.

• • • • • •●

These insurgencies live within the mysteries of a lateral physics in a distal universe just. Beyond our own and we who make the half twist toward it are subject to the absolute laws of an authority that some may call ancestors while others simply know as ineluctable—subatomic, built into the gene string, the double helix and surrounding molecules—the flower in the gun barrel, the die-in at the intersection, the leather glove on the single fist, rising, the knee on the turf and on the pitch, they are the soft twitch of the over-body—justice, the end of choice in the age of risk.

XLVIII

BADDHA KOṆĀSANA

BOUND ANGLE

340

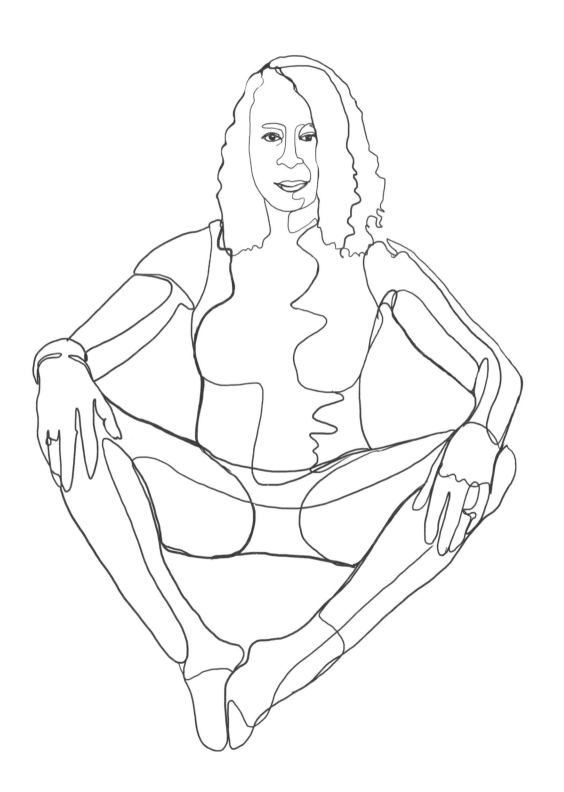

●······

Free me
of exemplar
or exception-
I sit as
myself
my thigh and hips
and give and space-
I sit as myself.

I'm not the lesson
the best
or lesser
story.
I sit as
myself.

I press my heels
into a casual
paradox
and hold
the bind.

I've got a mind
to live in this seat
I've got a spine
that holds
the intersections
that bolds its
way
through apparent
contradictions
that rises into
the unexpected
answers of
bones and pliancy

I hold all
that complexity
just fine.

I was born into
the natural tremors,
to thighs of
never resting
and I know that I am not one
river
nor do I answer to
a single name.

If you can't find
my calm,
call it my
currency,
a force beyond
damming
an answer
to no single name.

I will leave into
the waters
I will leave into
the waters

I believe

Into the never rested.

··· ● ···

I am the seated
kiss,
two continents at
uneasy peace,
the test of
the new migration,
the home
coming

in my body of
not visitor
and you
may name me
an invasion
or a destruction
of tectonic lift
but this is your
deep
shudder
and not my
geology
in your age of
ice and
shoulder
I am the
fingertip.

···· ● ··

You cannot sit
the warrior
out of me,
the wallop, grain
and center of
the heel left
sings like sharpened spears
and weighted arrows
and the right
is the bottom
of my throat,
and the
whale bone,
so when I sit,
I am riding—
a carve along
the mack,
a flash between
the timber
the gallop cry
at the arc of
where I squeeze.
I am never still.

You cannot break
or calm
or
sit me.

I lost my
one way
when my thighs
willed it
when this strange
adductor wisdom
sang an opening
so octave sweet
that I was forever augmented,
and I loved and
squeezed
in variety—
left my tongue and finger/toes
astonished by your
lush and sovereign
miracles of skin until these
sumptuous and accumulated
years of lostness
became
my finding.

We are the story
race, sons and daughters
of center force
pressed out of
opposites
into pages
and sword arc of goddesses,
lotus,
leaf and open palm,
claret of the spring,
shepherd staff and everlasting,
essence and minerals
spread across
this variegated earth.

The truth is in
our heels
and the void
between them,
of a friction
from the darkness—
a combustion
and its voice.

XLIX

JĀNU ŚĪRṢĀSANA

HEAD TO KNEE

346

●······

I fold into
the truth
of my interior,
past the sternum doubts—
into a divine shade,
a cooling confidence
toward this abdomen intrinsic,
the starting belly,
never lost,
a fierce haven
of my proud line
and resting gravity.

·●·····

What if my body
forms an
alliance with a
history
I have never
heard?

Should I follow—
lean down into
the darkness
of a blood earth
just below my knee,
take my hip
into the ache
of an extermination trail
by land and rail
and sea
feel the man
woman child end
of a once and forever family
though named
savage/slave/invader
instead of this?

What is this abrasion
that pulls me
to my shin,
will I ignore it—
hold my upright
take the center—

or listen in?

··●····

To know this tone along
my limbs
is to live in
the basic magic
of the empathies,
a chordal fluency
stretched along
my hamstrings
that bells the body
while the head
is left to wander.

I trust my mind
of skin
that listens for me
and leave
my thoughts to
a lesser story.

I am an instrument.

······•······

Just below
my patella hough
the ground has rung
a "never again ".

The strings
are keens
and my knees
are chambers
for my legs
to send
to my hips and ankles.

I trust these warnings of earth and eye
and tremors and tremors—
a "now" is here
a "now" is here.

I make my lean
to take my action
a "now" is here
a "now" is here.

· · · · ● · ·

I descend deep
past the
fear body—
the twitch
tendon strings
of the
demagogue instrument
into the original plain
where sound and wind
sing for distance
and I am one
with all these
spacious things.

Down into my
valley bones
beneath the frenzy
and all its stratum
set me long
like capillaries
in limb and solitude

I am the river
mineral long
at the shore of it
forehead resting
bottom to the glory

renunciate

expanse unto myself

I have left the nation capture
to find this range of skin
and all
it's
open borders.

· · · · ·●·

These are the
muscles of
the finding-
at the crossings of
my heels
and appearance
of your hands-
we are the
pose of a
common circumstance
of infinite extension
and not much
height
we live the weight
together
and thought this
was born alone
but we have stretched,
at near collapse
into an accidental
union
and how your bones
at involuntary test
belong to mine
despite the stations
they have set
for us
we are at
the low glance
of a liminal entangle
blind horizon
I see you on my skin
our sweat is
not so different
though our breath
and pavements
were separated
by design.

You and I
are sprawling
into nearness
at these
unexpected intersections.

We are the first revolution
here at the
long told

sliver of light.

· · · · · ·●

(For Lily)

I make my belonging
at two shores
though you see me
at the one.

My forehead knows
these places
the dunes and estuaries
of my western leg
and the eastern
of the salt marshes
and newly drowning coasts
as if the very waters
below my knee
advance in restitution
for the sins
of my fathers.

Mine is the
panorama reach
and a view
to resolution
a simultaneous
second sight
that lifts both horizons
toward the double
wisdoms
of my interior
and I see you
wanting a
single answer
to me,

to justify your shore

but I am the strand
and end
to your simplicity
a new hope
for a lost country
in a body
finely bent
for navigation.

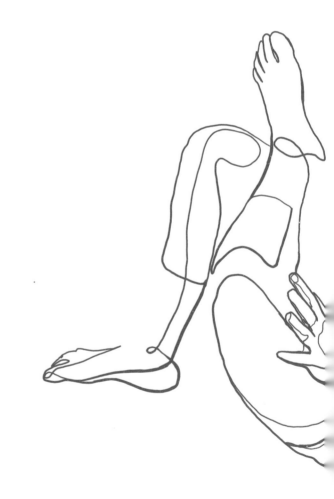

L

SŪCIRANDHRĀSANA

EYE OF THE NEEDLE

355

●······

This is the pose
called
"keep surprising my muscles
while I hug myself".

which is why
they usually save it

'til the end.

•●·····

I will not abandon
the pain of
these discoveries,
I will pull them in,
stretch my knowing,
reach through my
many little
endings
toward a tougher innocence,
a durable peace
and a

necessary ache.

·· • · · · ·

I am ready to enter
the tangle
to wrap my wrists
around my strings
and mysteries
and pull the taut
to tender.

I am set to
listen
to the snags
as they unwind
with such
fine resistance
until my dormant tones
of rage and tears
untwining revelation

finds its singing.

· · · ● · · ·

We are the people
who reach for
the eye of the dawn
though you forced
our welted backs
onto boarding school
beds.

We kept our tongues
deep in our throats
where you could not
hear the language
swimming there.

We made our thighs
strong
by pulling the
morning
toward them.

We tucked our bodies
into a survival
knot
that you could not
untwist.

We stretched our fingers
toward the fire
and this light
threads now
the narrow open spaces
like summer
on dead winter ground.

The occupation stories
are coming to their feet,
we have stretched them
ready
until we strike
the earth
like hided sticks
and bring
a rising.

·····●··

As I lay
I squeeze
the air and earth
into place
through the compass
of
my leg.

My body is
the first realm
of my seeing
and I am a
supreme instrument
of faith and navigation.

But the world
is blind to me
stumbles its
many mistakes
across
my daily paths
litters with visual
indulgence
of such spread
that I am often banished
to this clutter horizon
of such swift hazard-
a life of labyrinth

and while I could succumb,

I am living in
this hero
of a vessel
and it is outward in me
past their abyss
and blind interior
and into my better senses
and a different body,
out beyond the limits
of their witness.

......•.

I.
I am the accumulation
of distance in
estrangement to
my very skin,
a fallow landscape
of muscle earth
and I've lived past
the violations
that put me here
into this vast and slender
numbing accommodation-
a breathing testament,
a will of quiescence.

And so I passed.
And if I were a prayer,
it ended.

II.
I am no longer good with the bargain.

III.
I am more than empty ground.

IV.
This body
this biology-
not a whisper
but a magnificent
petulant grace
of such staying—
against all sins
of abandonment
so I pull these stalks
of limbs
toward the passage
of my throat
and the wind
I'm going to carry
into rain

I'm bracing

it stings

This is my body
I'm placing my
knees
near my thumbs
and pulling
my way back in—

This is my body
bently embracing
my (common fibular) nerve.

This is my body.

· · · · · ·•

I am the body
and the cradler
a necessity of double duty
low-
back to the earth-
where sights often fail
and survivors
count their breath.

These are my peoples
whispering commands
pulling ourselves tight
to each other
hidden by design-
a concentration
so hard
that the total of us
will not fall.

We live along
each other's
blood pulsing chests
and there are comforts in
these human ways
that colonizers
must not remember
distances they
choose to keep
and we mean to close.

Let us sing to
each other's limbs
so that we cannot be
severed
and tangle
our way forward
like pliancy
and a weapon
of thorns.

Let us smell
the chlorophyll
in our veins
and duplicate
the weeds of our nature
that laughed us
back to earth
despite our many losses,
our many many losses
and still counting.

We are not their bodies
we are our own
and our cradlers
as I—
am my witness.

LI

APĀNĀSANA

KNEE TO CHEST

362

●······   ·●·····

We who live
in yours
make ourselves
into our
own spaces,
pull our doubleness
back into one,
live within these
tight sanctuaries
of tender fingers
over overstretched
and wounded knees
and tend
with no explanations.

Let me take
myself
into the ways
of solitude and
reconstruction.

Let me take myself

home.

Called my limbs,
like routes and prayers
into this redemption
of the abdomen spine
and I am the end
of the two migration
I am three
and often four
pulled in tight
so that's my name
my many lives
that's my name
I wont for less
and core
my tight

That's my name
that's my name
routes and prayers
to that's my name
that's my name.

One tug toward
a calibration
of the aft
who live within me and
the descendants.

I've made
this spine
a home

for all of us.

We will not
be your people
of perpetual forgiveness,
we will raise our arms,
shake these ankles clean
and fold our bodies
toward unrelenting fierce,
forever standing.

. . . . ● . .

Sing expanse,
sing your mysteries
into my tibia instruments
until I take my grip
of the chordal plane,
surrender my stillness
and become your willing
and deeper chamber.

· · · · ·●·

I pulled deep into
the below
where the earth
is listening.

I have learned,
despite my bravado
that I am only
saving myself.

This is a planet
that takes her time
grieves her losses
and makes a healing.

I am no one's master.

I am only saving myself.

· · · · · ·●

This,
at last,
is my divinity,
a contraction into light,
a founding
the prime antithesis
of an exponential lie –
this is me –
a fine and spiral universe
the winding answer
to the flat dimension
and monotony of force
this is the wending
tuck –
Imagination
the supple universe
at dawn—

my divinity.

LII

ŚAVĀSANA

CORPSE

368

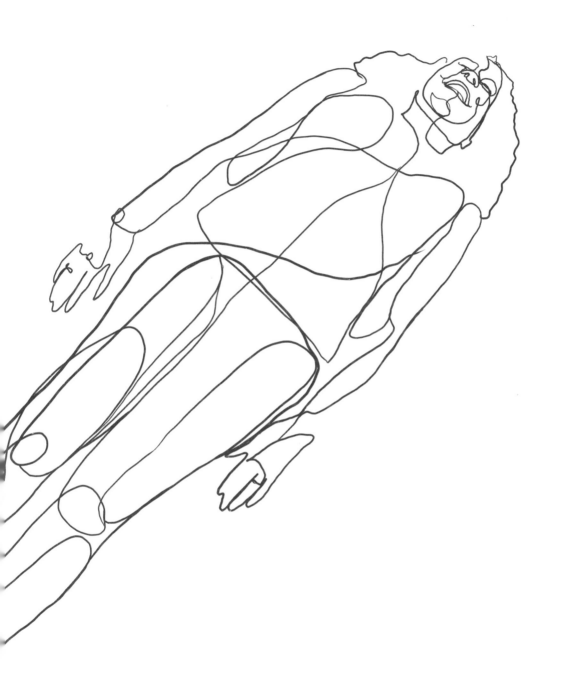

●••••••

I surrender to
the long affiliations
my back body stretched
upon the
story mounds,
my clavicle frets
bound to all
those strings
that make me
a perfect instrument
to the narrators
of my kin
and I am breathing

so much stolen horizon

and still this ground
is song to never

I am breathing.

•●•••••

This is my
blessing
of the eyes closed
no face to
try to
figure out,
no subtle tone
to miss again
no hints and gestures,
brutal lights
of the overhead,
fire alarms
to make me mute
no personal spaces
to measure out,
no body language
I still can't see
I still can't see
and it takes me out
and sends me down
until I sleep
but this is better

this is rest
this is rest
this is rest.

•• • • • • •

Lain, like the fitted bed sheet smooth, with 20 rooms left on my shift and six days until rest.

Lain, to 5 million yards of tie, with sweat on every spike and winding rail and still waiting.

Lain, like graded vines at eight feet distance in even rows
and an exhaustion of workers deftly culling without the wage, the clinics or the welcoming

generosity relegated to the tender plump of grape.

Lain, like perfect rivets at the dockyard torch divinities from the fingers of those
great, great grandsons of Fulani, Wolof, Mandinka and Jola still dreaming of an open deck.

Lain, like a billion backs of prayer, spines conjuring the song of springs against the enemies
of water

minds and bones in tight defense.

Lain Like the needed pause, the exhalation while the changing takes my skin and I've become

the revolution

that I have never been.

This is the time
of the dying,
the brief and floating
distance of gravity
and the broken leaf,
the necessity of earth
and these limbs
I take in the compost
and return.

This is the deep
and the pitch
in my chest
where my comforts
are silent
and my breath
is my only prayer.

This is my falling away
a descent into suspension
and the tears
that carry me
the tears that carry me

and the next thread of light.

The thread of light
pressed beneath
the tongue
of my sleep
gives a word
to the length of my spine
and I am not afraid.

This sacred boundary
of skin,
kin above accumulations
to facia
must be stretched
and broken
each day.

And so, I
open
even on my
back
I open and
sing the whisper
caught between my ribs
until I am the word
that I remember
and only then
to rise.

I lay and only
then to
rise.

. . . . . ●.

This is where
we get
to do

the being part.

. . . . . .●

My back knuckle body
likes the floor
with all
its certainties,
a good earth,
a durability of bones
and the rumor
of a familiar song.

I'm waiting
to meet myself

and it may take a while.

LIII

TĀḌĀSANA

MOUNTAIN

374

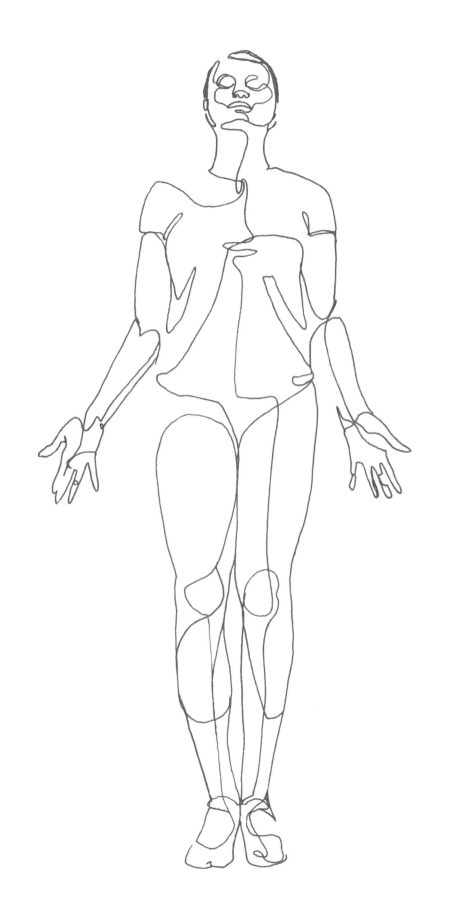

······· ●

Above supremacy
are the range of us
angles and slopes
spectrums of loams and
all the layering cold logic
at our heights
warming to the
glacial rivers
and the catch of lakes.

We are the masters
of settlement,
a potency of grit,
no fan of posture,
we are the power
of the purest rank,
the discipline
of the deeper listening
the landforms among you,
the original –
reborn
dwarfing
the flickering preen
that dances itself out
below.

THE YOGA MODELS

THE 365 REVOLUTIONS TEAM

Lucas Smiraldo,
Author

Lucas Smiraldo is a poet, produced playwright and former Poet Laureate for the City of Tacoma where he launched the grassroots based "Laureate Listening Project". 365 Revolutions is his third, and most ambitious, published book which was preceded by *"365 Revolutions: Lunar Cycle"* and *"The Thing That Gathers"*. Mr. Smiraldo's work, *"Voice of the Americas"* debuted as both a live stage production/ CD launch with sound score by Wrick Wolff at Theater on the Square in 2008. He conceived, and was lead writer, for a touring show produced by Tacoma Arts Live, titled *"Eleven Days in the Life of Dr. King"* in collaboration with poets Chimaera and Antonio Edwards, which has reached over 50,000 youth in Western Washington over the course of multiple tours. He lives in Tacoma, Washington where his wife, Claudette Evans, (pictured on the cover) a yoga teacher and certified Sanskrit teacher has converted their living room into a vibrant remote studio space. By day, Lucas is an Equity Policy Analyst for the City of Tacoma's Office of Equity and Human Rights which continues to inform his creative work.

Lovetta Reyes-Cairo,
Illustrator

Lovetta Reyes-Cairo grew up in an artistic family and has spent countless wonderful hours doing art. She graduated from Brigham Young University and also studied at an independent art school, Beaux-Arts Academy, in Provo, UT. For Lovetta, art heals and allows for exploration and expression of feelings as few other things can, and she wants to share that with others. Her work is both personal and universal, often featuring the human figure and exploring ideas of spirituality, healing, balance, beauty, and love. Lovetta enjoys practicing yoga and often turns to it for centering herself and personal growth.

"I have truly felt honored to illustrate so many beautiful people through this book. Attempting to capture these complex and diverse identities using simple lines has opened my eyes and mind. I have been able to more deeply see and honor the divine in each of us."

**Kaitlyn Bowman,
Project Director**

This project has many moving parts including website development, yoga model recruitment, marketing and outreach and many other components, which have all been headed up by Kaitlyn. Kait owns a traveling business combining her passions of photography, yoga, and travel called Wandering Soul Collective. The collective is a collaboration of light perceiving light in order to inspire and nurture minds, bodies, and spirits, through reflectional imagery, harmony of breath and body, and tangible tools for healing. She also travels the globe with a women's yoga trip company called Work Your Wild, capturing the essence evoked by sisterhood within nature and illuminates the authentic divinity that resides within them.

**Uchenna Baker, PhD,
Leadership Embodied Forward**

Dr. Baker is currently Vice President For Student Affairs and Dean of Students at Fairleigh Dickinson University. She earned an M.Ed. in counseling psychology and a B.A. in English and sociology, both from Rutgers University. She completed her PhD in educational policy with a focus on urban education through a joint program of Rutgers University and the New Jersey Institute of Technology. Her dissertation research was titled "An Ontological and Phenomenological Model of Leadership: Igniting Individual and Collective Transformation and Catalyzing Educational Reform."

Dr. Baker was the 2016 recipient of the Illinois Qualitative Dissertation Award presented by the International Congress of Qualitative Inquiry at the University of Illinois at Urbana-Champaign. In her research, she chronicles her own personal journey in leadership as an African-American educator and student affairs practitioner. Dr. Baker has presented her award-winning research at national and international conferences, through self-led university workshops, invited talks, conferences and classroom presentations. She continues to center her work on leadership and the intersections between personal and organizational purpose through her training program, LEAP or Leading, Ethically, Authentically, and with Purpose.

RESOURCES

**Michelle Cassandra Johnson
(Forward) and Skill in Action**

Michelle's work focuses on living skillfully
while taking action to make change for
the collective good. She has created a
200hr and 300hr yoga teacher training
program focused on the intersection of
social justice and yoga, and subsequently
authored her book, Skill in Action:
Radicalizing Your Yoga Practice to Create
a Just World, and to travel the world
teaching about what it means to center
justice in yoga and wellness spaces.

Skill in Action: Radicalizing Your
Yoga Practice to Create a Just World
asks readers to explore the deeply
transformational practice of yoga and
become social change agents so that
they can create a world that is just for
all. The book explores liberation for
ourselves and others, while asking us
to engage in our own agency, whether
that manifests as activism, volunteer
work, or changing our relationships with
others and ourselves. Here is the link
to Michelle's Skill in Action website:

skill-in-action.com

Native Strength Revolution

In a quest to invite diverse photographs
that are now transformed into illustrations
for this book, I learned about an
extraordinary program focusing on wellness
for Native American and indigenous people
titled "Native Strength Revolution' founded
by Kate Herrera Jenkins. Native Strength
Revolutions equips a new generation of
Indigenous healers through leadership
training and yoga certification and makes
that access possible through online
learning options for emerging leaders and
healers who may live in remote locations
throughout North America. Many of the
yoga models have joined the 365 team
as a result of of this partnership and
several members have lent their voices
to the first volume of the audio book.

nativestrengthrevolution.org

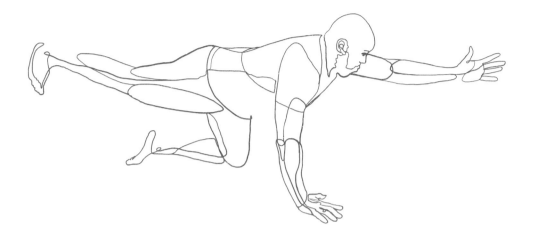

Litehouse Wellness

We also want to recognize the extraordinary work of Litehouse Wellness, and of "Broga" stewarded by Sherrie Doucette who has sustained a loving platform for black men and people of color within the healing practices of yoga. Her nonprofit helps to guide African American men toward wellness, toward healing arts, and prevention practices, preventative health education, and plant-based lifestyle coaching.

litehousewellness.org

OTHER 365 REVOLUTION CREATIONS

365 Revolutions: A People's Ensemble with Original Sound Score, Volume 1

This audio creation features a compelling and diverse ensemble of voices who bring their lived experiences into passionate readings pieces from the book. Performed to original sound scores from three composers.

365 Yoga Illustration Collection: Revolutionary Bodies in Motion

Possibly the most diverse collection of yoga bodies in motion that has been gathered into a single collection of high-end single line illustrations. Created by Lovetta Reyes-Cairo in collaboration with the 365 team. Derived from yoga models from multiple racial, gender, orientation, body, and ability identities, each model contributed the use of their image in exchange for full and free access to their illustrations.

365 Revolutions Illustrated Literary Prints

Literary prints that integrate poems from the book with the line illustrations of Lovetta Reyes-Cairo.

Text: Lucas Smiraldo
Illustrations: Lovetta Reyes-Cairo
Proofreading: Claudette Evans
Book design: Cleber de Campos
Typefaces: SM Maxeville Construct, Helvetica
Paper cover: 3mm ESKA Grey Board
Paper inside: 80gsm Milan Neutral paper
Spine cloth: JHT-0090 Orange Cloth
Lithography: locolor
Printing and binding: Artron Art Center
Publisher: Auricle Press

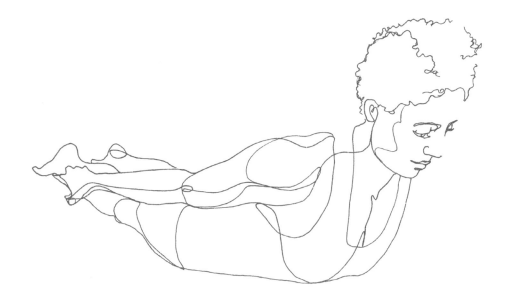

To right myself
and
become my
own name.